THE SEVEN
TYPES OF
SPIRIT
GUIDE

Praise for
The Seven Types of Spirit Guide

'Yamile has opened the door and invites us into the beautiful and loving realm of spirit helpers and guides in this grounded and gorgeous book. Reading it will reassure you at the deepest level that you are loved, supported, and watched over every minute of your life. Peace washes over you as Yamile helps you connect with your guides.'
SONIA CHOQUETTE, BEST-SELLING AUTHOR OF *ASK YOUR GUIDES*

'Yamile Yemoonyah's book is clear, comprehensive, and easy to follow. As an initiated Santeria Priestess, I especially appreciate her unique multicultural approach. If you are ready to make a deeper connection with your spirit guides, this is the book for you!'
CAROLYN WILKINS, PSYCHIC MEDIUM, REIKI HEALER, AND PRIESTESS OF YEMAYA

'As we evolve spiritually, it's so important to keep our minds open and broaden our perceptions. I really feel Yamile's book has the key to unlock so much within us to reveal a greater understanding of who we are on a soul level and appreciate just how much we are loved by the universe and all those beings that share our space.'
TONY STOCKWELL, PSYCHIC MEDIUM AND AUTHOR

'This is an absolutely fantastic book that will help you to call in and activate your spiritual support team. If you want to connect with your personal team of guides and helpers, I cannot recommend this book enough.'
REBECCA CAMPBELL, BEST-SELLING AUTHOR OF *LIGHT IS THE NEW BLACK* AND THE *WORK YOUR LIGHT ORACLE CARDS*

'What I love most about Yamile's work is that it reminds us that we are all worthy of having a spirit guide, and ultimately she teaches us to know them too!'

KYLE GRAY, BEST-SELLING AUTHOR OF *ANGEL NUMBERS* AND *RAISE YOUR VIBRATION*

'This book is absolutely perfect for those wanting to know more about spirit guides. Yes, we all have them and Yamile has made it clear what types of guides one may have and how they are accessible to all of us. An incredible read!'

CLAIRE STONE, BESTSELLING AUTHOR OF *THE FEMALE ARCHANGELS*

'Yamile eloquently shares her knowledge of spirit guides. She shows us that everyone has a spirit guide, and how we can learn to communicate with them. I love that she has included an entire chapter on Nature Spirits too!'

KAREN KAY, AUTHOR OF *ORACLE OF THE FAIRIES* AND *MESSAGES FROM THE MERMAIDS*

'A practical guide to accessing and understanding the world of the Spirit Guide. Yamile writes with the passion of a practitioner whilst demonstrating a genuine account of experiential mediumship. I commend Yamile on authoring her first book and I recommend it to all seekers of the truth.'

ANN TREHERNE, CHAIR, ARTHUR CONAN DOYLE CENTRE, EDINBURGH, AND AUTHOR OF *ARTHUR AND ME*

THE SEVEN
TYPES OF
SPIRIT
GUIDE

How to Connect and Communicate
with Your Cosmic Helpers

Yamile Yemoonyah

HAY HOUSE

Carlsbad, California • New York City
London • Sydney • New Delhi

Published in the United Kingdom by:
Hay House UK Ltd, The Sixth Floor, Watson House
54 Baker Street, London W1U 7BU
Tel: +44 (0)20 3927 7290; Fax: +44 (0)20 3927 7291; www.hayhouse.co.uk

Published in the United States of America by:
Hay House Inc., PO Box 5100, Carlsbad, CA 92018-5100
Tel: (1) 760 431 7695 or (800) 654 5126
Fax: (1) 760 431 6948 or (800) 650 5115; www.hayhouse.com

Published in Australia by:
Hay House Australia Ltd, 18/36 Ralph St, Alexandria NSW 2015
Tel: (61) 2 9669 4299; Fax: (61) 2 9669 4144; www.hayhouse.com.au

Published in India by:
Hay House Publishers India, Muskaan Complex,
Plot No.3, B-2, Vasant Kunj, New Delhi 110 070
Tel: (91) 11 4176 1620; Fax: (91) 11 4176 1630; www.hayhouse.co.in

Tradepaper ISBN: 978-1-78817-376-6
E-book ISBN: 978-1-78817-379-7
Audiobook ISBN: 978-1-78817-553-1

Interior illustrations: Shutterstock

Printed and bound by CPI Group (UK) Ltd, Croydon CR0 4YY

I dedicate this book to my parents, the ones who gave me life and, more importantly, the ones who raised me and, to this day, lovingly support me in all I do.

CONTENTS

SPIRIT GUIDED

Spirit has guided my life right from the start, even though I didn't always realize it. To be clear, when I talk about Spirit I mean the universal force that's behind all creation. You can also call it God, the Universe, the Creator, the force, or any other term that makes sense to you. Being guided by Spirit doesn't make me special. We all have that privilege. Like me, you may not realize it, but this guidance is available to you at all times. It comes in the form of spirit guides, who act as the Universe's ambassadors. In this book I'll teach you how to connect and communicate with these guides so they can help you create a better future for yourself, for others, and for the world at large. But first let me back up and tell you how I started detecting the influence of spirit guides in my own life. Then I want to recount how this changed me forever and how your guides can do the same for you.

I grew up in a non-religious household with two parents who embraced science over any kind of spiritual belief. This meant that I didn't have much exposure to knowledge that could have explained what happened in my mid-twenties and altered the course of my life. At the time, I was living in Germany and clueless about my direction in life. I knew that I felt a calling deep down in my heart, but I didn't realize what it meant or what to do about it. I felt stuck, depressed, and often wondered if something was wrong with me. I even considered checking myself into a psychiatric hospital because I perceived myself as broken and was looking for a way to fix myself. Looking back, I understand that this was the start of my journey to becoming a spirit guide medium. I was about to learn how to deliver messages to those who hadn't (yet) learnt to communicate with their cosmic helpers themselves.

About one month after my 26th birthday, I woke up at around 4 a.m. to find a man I'd never seen before standing in the doorway of my bedroom. He was wearing jeans but no shirt, shoes, or socks. His hair was short and black, his skin was brown, and he looked as though he was of indigenous South American ancestry, just like me. I stared at him and he stared back. Then, from out of nowhere, he produced a glowing red orb the size of a baseball that hovered above his upturned and outstretched right hand. It looked like a tiny version of the sun at dusk, right before it disappears below the horizon. He threw it over to me and I still remember the impact it made as it landed on the bed right next to me. Next thing I knew, I was opening my eyes the next morning and wondering what had just happened.

Two days later, I boarded a train to attend a shamanism workshop in Berlin that I'd signed up for weeks before. It had been organized by the Foundation for Shamanic Studies, founded by Michael Harner, an anthropologist who had influenced the rise of Neo-Shamanism, a Westernized form of various traditional shamanic traditions. I'd just started becoming interested in my Colombian roots and wanted to learn more about the spiritual traditions of my indigenous ancestors. On that five-hour train ride to Berlin, I told my friend Bianca, who was accompanying me, what had happened two nights before and we wondered what it all meant.

The next morning, after arriving at the event location, we were eager to get started. Our teacher, Paul Uccusic, a seasoned shamanic practitioner of over 30 years, had everyone sit in a big circle and introduce themselves. Then he told us we were about to learn how to connect with our spirit guides by going on a trip to the spirit world. After explaining how to do this, he told us that when we met our guide for the very first time, they would often transfer energy to us to help raise our vibration. This would either be by giving us a loving hug or, sometimes, by handing us a glowing red orb.

I gasped and nudged my friend, who looked at me with eyes wide. We'd both realized that the man who had showed up in my bedroom two days earlier was one of my spirit guides!

I don't remember much of the rest of the workshop other than I felt that I'd entered a new world that had been hidden from me before. Intuitively, I sensed that a door had been opened and that I was to embark on a journey that would have a big impact on my life.

At the end of the workshop, many of the participants were ready to dive deeper into the subject through follow-up courses on healing, soul retrieval, and other shamanic practices. Paul answered their questions about the specifics, but what I'll never forget is that first he told us that he'd already taught us everything we needed. He'd helped us connect with our guides, and they would do the rest.

Our guides are our real teachers. They're aware of what our soul came to do in this incarnation on Mother Earth and can guide us on our spiritual path and in daily life. All we have to do is learn how to connect with these cosmic helpers. They can then assist us in aligning with our higher self, discovering our gifts and talents, gaining clarity about our purpose, and receiving general mentorship and guidance. I took no other courses with the foundation and Paul has since passed. But with this book I hope to continue his legacy and enable you to connect with your own guides. Then they can teach you whatever you need to learn so you, too, can live a conscious life guided by Spirit.

Spirit guide blessings

My spirit guides have brought many blessings into my life and yours can do the same for you. However, if you've never learnt how to communicate with them, it can take a long time to recognize these blessings, let alone act on them to improve your life. I want to help you fast-track that process and enjoy the benefits as soon as possible.

Over the years, I've had many more encounters with spirits. In my own home I've met three aliens who looked as though they'd stepped straight out of a Hollywood movie. A friendly nature spirit once 'possessed' me at a campfire in the woods. A troll popped out of the earth in front of me in Barcelona and a light being appeared in the volcanic desert of the Canary Islands. Besides this short collection, I have many more spirit stories from the 20 years since that fateful night in the year 2000.

I've enjoyed these crazy adventures and over time they've helped me understand my mission and purpose in life. However, in the beginning they didn't seem to have any real implications for my life because I didn't know how to interpret them. I had no control over them and couldn't predict when they would happen. I only talked about them to a few select people who were also on a spiritual path. I was busy trying to figure out what I wanted to do with my life once I 'grew up.' In the meantime I worked as a barista, pre-edited documentaries, sold cell phone contracts, worked in customer support centers, and was a hostess at international fairs. In 2006, I discovered that I could sell my art on the Internet. At the same time I was struggling with the impact of my adoption. Trust and identity issues ruled my life and contributed to not being able to find my place in the world.

It took me 15 years after that first encounter with what I now know to be my ancestral guide to realize that connecting with spirit guides was a gift that could be developed and used to help others. In 2015, the incidents increased, but they were different now. It wasn't just about random spirits popping up here and there anymore. During that summer there were multiple instances when I was out and about with friends and would feel drawn to a person sitting close by. I wasn't sure why, but the air would energize and thicken around me. Then, if I let my mind go blank, I'd sense an ancestor or maybe an animal spirit around the person. I'd also receive information about them – a tidbit from their childhood, information on their struggle with an emotional issue, or the reason for the fight they had just had with their partner. I thought this was an interesting new development, but I still didn't get it.

Only when I discovered mediumship as taught in the Spiritualist tradition did the pieces fall into place. I started watching a TV show called *Monica the Medium* and got hooked. The way she described how she'd discovered that she was a medium reminded me of my own journey. Feeling drawn to random people, the air getting thicker, and information coming through all sounded familiar. The difference was that I didn't see dead people, I saw other types of spirit. Still, this was a major revelation and one that I needed to investigate. So I signed up for an online mediumship class and read every single book I could find on the topic. It was like coming home and I finally knew what I wanted to do with my life! The cherry on top came when my mother mentioned that when I was about five years old, my great-uncle, who had been into UFOs, had told her I was a natural medium. A year later, my guides asked me to set up a website and start doing spirit guide readings. The rest is history.

The life challenges you're struggling with might look different from mine. Whatever they are, your spirit guides can help you work through them and live a life that makes you happy and fulfilled.

Here are some of the blessings you can expect after connecting with them:

Alignment with your higher self

Your spirit guides can help moderate the fear-based ego and empower your true self to run the show instead. The result is a state that artists and athletes call 'being in the flow' and your life will unfold with more ease and clarity.

Increased trust in the Universe and yourself

Fear can only rule you if you lack trust. Once your higher self is in charge, you'll gain more confidence in yourself and have more faith in the Universe, yourself, and your spirit guides.

The discovery of gifts and talents

We all have undiscovered gifts and talents that can bring a multitude of blessings into our lives. Your guides know what yours are and can help you unearth them for your highest good and to serve others.

Clarity about your life's purpose

Do you wonder what you came here to do during this incarnation? Your guides can point you in the right direction and assist you in fulfilling your life's mission step by step.

General mentorship and guidance

Your guides are also available for any other support you need. They can help you create more abundance in your life and build better relationships. They're also happy to show you the underlying spiritual principles that can assist you in designing a better future for yourself and others.

What to expect from this book

This is the first-ever exploration of the different kinds of cosmic helper that have communicated with shamans, mediums, priests, and everyday people across cultures and throughout human history. I'm approaching the topic from a culturally inclusive perspective. I wrote the book not only to give you information, but also practical tactics to apply to your own spiritual work. Through it, I hope to change the way you think about, respect, and interact with spirit guides.

Through my work delivering messages from and answering questions about spirit guides every day, I experience first hand that there are many people hungry to learn more about these cosmic helpers. From my interactions with my clients and online community, I'm intimately familiar with what it is people wonder about. The common questions I'm asked are: What exactly is a spirit guide? Who is my spirit guide? Can I have more than one spirit guide? Do evil spirits exist and how do I avoid them? How can I connect and communicate with my guides? Am I making it all up or was this a real experience? Can my spirit guides help me develop my spiritual abilities? How can my spirit guides help me find my purpose?

I relate very well, as my interest in spirit guides goes much deeper than my business. I was born in Colombia to an indigenous woman of the Emberá, a tribe that relies on its shamans for advice and healing. When I was 18 months old, a loving Dutch family who, as already mentioned, didn't believe in the supernatural or subscribe to any kind of spiritual belief, adopted me and raised me in Germany. As a child, I already had a connection to the spirit world, but no words to talk about it. That was until my ancestral guide physically appeared in my bedroom and took me on a journey that transformed my life, giving me a sense of purpose, belonging, and grace. I want the same for you!

So, this book not only explains what spirit guides are, but explores the specific characteristics, gifts, and challenges that each type of guide brings with them. It also features an extended version of my popular viral quiz to help you discover which types of spirit guide you have and how best to communicate with them. Best of all, it reassures you that you don't need to be a shaman, witch, priest, or other professional spirit worker, or have any special abilities to do this. All you need is an open heart and mind, along with a healthy sense of curiosity.

The book is organized into three parts:

Part I lays the foundation by explaining the key terms and giving you a quick introduction to the seven different types of spirit guide. It also explains why you may not have succeeded in connecting with your cosmic helpers (yet). Then it moves on to the benefits and dangers of working with spirit guides and gets you in the right mindset to consciously connect with them. At the end, you get to take the quiz that helps you identify the types of guide that make up your personal team of cosmic helpers. From there, you're ready to learn more!

Part II has seven chapters, one on each of the seven types of guide: deities, ancestors, ascended masters, nature spirits, animal guides, star beings, and angels. Each chapter dives into the specific characteristics, gifts, and challenges of that particular guide. It also explores what having them around says about you, and shares examples, both past and present, of humans from various cultures and spiritual traditions working with that type of guide. This section serves as a primer, helping you become familiar with your spirit guide team members and allowing you to better identify spirit guides as you encounter them. You also get to create your unique communication style to converse with your cosmic helpers.

Part III reassures you that anyone can communicate with their spirit guides and outlines how to create a ritual to connect with the specific guides you're working with.

You can then use your spirit guide connection to further your spiritual development, manifest your dreams, live your purpose, and make the world a better place for yourself and others.

Are you ready to begin?

～

PART I

LAYING
THE
FOUNDATION

Chapter 1

ARE YOU READY?

Looking back, I can see the thread that weaves itself through my life and led me to connect with my spirit guides and become a spirit guide medium. When I was born, my Colombian birth mother was only 16 years old. After a year of struggling to provide for me, she gave me up for adoption. Foster parents took care of me for a few months before my Dutch parents adopted me and raised me in Germany. As is true for many adoptees, especially for cross-cultural ones, not knowing where I'd come from caused me to develop identity issues. Despite having a loving family, something seemed to be missing from my life because of my unknown past. Even though I tried, it was hard to focus on the future and figure out what I wanted to do with my life without knowing more about my roots. Nowadays, I know there's also a positive side to having a flexible identity and it can even be a blessing. Letting go of our rigid perception of self, including our expectations and fears, is the biggest hurdle for most of us when it comes to spirit guide communication. However, as a young person, I hadn't developed that wisdom yet.

I was one of the lucky ones (not all adoptees are). My parents are the best, and they love me and support me 100 percent in all I do. Still, growing up in a Dutch family in small-town Germany during the 1980s was sometimes tough. On the outside, I had an ideal upbringing. On the inside, I had many insecurities. One reason for them was that I had no role models who looked like me, neither among my family members, nor the local community nor the media. In fact, I was one of only three children of color in my entire school. I hated my looks and thought I was ugly, even though people told me otherwise all the time. My insecurities also stemmed from indirect and even open racism. One early winter's evening when I was 12 years old, just as it was getting dark, I was waiting for my mother to pick me up after an afternoon activity when a man rounded the corner and threatened to kill me if I didn't go 'back where I came from.' I'm sure you can imagine how scary, confusing, and hurtful that was.

That same year, I also had a spiritual experience that made a huge impact on me and shows how, bit by bit, my spiritual awareness grew. My parents took my brother and me on a trip to the United States. The minute the plane touched down on the landing strip, I knew I was home, even though I'd never been there before and couldn't explain this odd sensation.

Subtle and inexplicable spiritual experiences like this would happen throughout my childhood and teens. I remember walking through the woods as a 17-year-old, following my intuition down a path that took me off the trail and through some bushes and ended overlooking a meadow. I stopped, and the air thickened and energized around me. A sensation of peace and sacredness settled in my heart and I took a few deep breaths. I didn't understand what was happening, but felt blessed and peaceful.

As a university student, I was still struggling with insecurities and sometimes full-blown depression. I was desperately searching for meaning, purpose, and my place in the world. At this low point, my spirit guides decided that I was ready for them to enter my life. Without realizing that they were behind it, I became obsessed with finding out more about my indigenous ancestry. After doing lots of research online, I found out there were about 100 different indigenous communities in Colombia. My next discovery showed that I was likely of Emberá descent. This indigenous community lives in the rainforests and the western valleys of the Andes on the west coast of Colombia. They've preserved much of their traditional language and many of their customs and spiritual traditions. Even in the face of being caught in the middle of the fights between the government, the guerrillas, and the paramilitary groups in their area.

I developed a deep desire to connect with my ancestors on a spiritual level. And the more I dug into this topic, the more signs, symbols, and synchronicities showed up in my life. It all culminated in that fateful night when my ancestral guide appeared in my bedroom in full physical form, as described earlier. After this incident, my life changed forever. Something had shifted inside me. For the first time, I symbolically sensed solid ground under my feet. It didn't matter that I couldn't remember my birth mother and father; I now felt connected with and supported by my ancestors on a spiritual level. This enabled me to learn that everything I'd perceived as negative and shameful about myself was in reality a gift. Once used to help others, that gift would bring enormous blessings into my life.

Everyone has their own insecurities to cope with and yours will be different from mine. However, whatever they may be, it's time to deal with them so you can shine your light for the world. Are you ready to meet your spirit guides so they can help heal those issues? If you are, they can also assist you in developing your spiritual abilities, finding inner peace, and succeeding in life.

The fact that you've picked up this book tells me something important about you. It shows me you're a lightworker, someone who is meant to make this world a better place for all by shining your light as brightly as possible. 'Shining your light' means using the innate skills, talents, and gifts you came here to share with the rest of us. If you don't like the term 'lightworker,' use something that's more to your liking. The point is your soul came here with a mission and you need to follow that calling to feel happy and fulfilled. As you're reading this book, you're not just a lightworker, but also a spirit worker. This means part of your destiny is to collaborate with the spirit world. Not necessarily in a professional sense as a shaman, medium, witch, or priestess (unless you feel called to do so). However, it's essential that you keep the channel to your spirit guides open so they can advise you throughout your life.

Your cosmic team

So, you have a mission to fulfill in this lifetime, but you don't have to do it on your own – you're part of a cosmic team. This team is comprised of several spirit guides of different types. Each has their own special way of helping you fulfill your soul's task. Such a cosmic team has at least three permanent members and some specialists who join for a limited time to accomplish certain tasks. They then leave to assist someone else. Everyone has at least one ancestor guide and one angel on their team. Who the others are depends on your past experiences as a soul and what you came here to do. Ancestor spirits, for example, help you create loving relationships in your life, while deities concern themselves more with the legacy you leave behind.

Your core team of heavenly helpers are the ones who stay with you your entire life. They're well aware of the soul contract you agreed to before you embarked on your trip to Earth. Their job is to help you unlock, unearth, and polish those parts of your soul that will have a positive impact on your own and other people's lives. They have the information you need to recognize your specific skills and talents and how to use them to make this world a more egalitarian, inclusive, and collaborative place.

I realize that you might think you're not special enough to have a team of spirit guides. Well, I don't agree! Why else would you be interested in spiritual topics, and spirit guides in particular? It's your soul guiding you to the things that are meaningful to you and that will further your spiritual growth. Your interests, hobbies, and desires always show you the way to fulfilling your soul's mission. Therefore, your wish to connect with your guides shows you're a soul who didn't just incarnate for your own pleasure and growth, but to raise the vibration of the planet. You do that by sharing your skills, gifts, and talents with the world. Your spirit guides are essential to that process, and on a deep soul level, you know that. Your life purpose is in fact part of a bigger mission that you and your guides are working on together. That's why it's vital for you to learn to connect and communicate with your team of heavenly helpers.

Still have doubts? That's your ego trying to tell you I can't possibly be talking about you. Well, I'm here to tell you that you don't need to be better looking, younger, richer, more educated, a perfect parent, or meditate every day before you can make a difference. You can be a lightworker and a spirit worker right now. You already are. Whatever insecurities are holding you back, they're in no way a sign that you don't have a spirit guide team and a mission to accomplish. In fact, your insecurities may be your secret weapon. Once transformed, they can become your strongest asset. We'll talk about that more later in this chapter. For now, I want you to know that your cosmic team is waiting for you. They want you to acknowledge their existence and work with them so they can help you fulfill your life's purpose by living with purpose every single day. I found that connecting with my spirit guides was the key to turning my life around. I discovered my gifts and started sharing them, fulfilling my mission and finding my place in the world. The same can happen for you!

You're reading this book now… That shows me you're almost ready. Ready to take the next step on your spiritual journey. Ready to step up and let your light shine, which is what lies at the core of your Earthly mission. This might take a different form for every one of us. We all need to find our individual expression, but letting our light shine is what it's all about. Unhealed wounds in our heart may be preventing us from living our full potential and shining our light. But our cosmic team can help us heal those wounds. Right underneath them lies the solution: the skills, talents, and gifts that will help us fulfill our mission. Are you ready to discover yours? But first, let's look at why you haven't managed to connect with your spirit guides yet.

Contacting your team

Why it's so hard to connect with our spirit guides

If you're like most of my students, you've already tried connecting with your heavenly helpers. There are many meditations on the Internet that promise to help you do so. However, since you're reading this book, you might not have succeeded. Why is it so many people fail? Here is the secret. It's not that our guides aren't there or don't want to answer our questions. In fact, they communicate with us all the time! The fault doesn't lie with them, but with us. We often stand in our own way. Here are the four main ways we block ourselves from getting the cosmic support we seek:

Reason #1: Our Western mindset gets in the way

Many values of Western society dominate the world at this moment in history and influence our daily lives, whether we live in the West or not. One of these values is what I call *scientific rationality*. It's the distinguishing mark of modern science. All of us are exposed to it every single day, even if we didn't study any of the exact sciences. It states that only what is perceivable with the five physical senses, that is measurable and repeatable, is real, and everything else isn't. And spiritual experiences do *not* always fall into this category. For this reason, our rational mind has learnt to view them as suspicious, imaginary, and discardable.

If you've ever done a guided meditation to connect with your guides, the following example might ring true for you. Let's assume you're trying to find your spirit guide's name during this meditation. With your mind's eye you see an image of a rose. Your intuition knows that this is a message from your guide telling you that their name is Rose. Your rational mind, however, wants proof. It questions everything, to the point where you become confused and start doubting your intuition. Soon you're dismissing the answer you've got from your guide and telling yourself that the meditation didn't work. Sound familiar?

Reason #2: Our own expectations sabotage us

As humans, we assume that our cosmic helpers communicate in the same way we do: either through the spoken word or through other forms of sensory input coming from the outside world. This is a false assumption. Spirit guides have their own language, and just like we can't expect a French person to reply to us in Italian, we need to adjust our expectations and learn their language. So don't expect a booming voice from heaven to give you the answer to all your problems. In fact, you might never externally *hear* your guide's voice or *see* what they look like. Instead, their messages might come as an inner knowing, a memory, a vision, or a dream. They can also come as signs, symbols, synchronicities, sudden insights, or vague intuitive feelings. These may not be what you were expecting, but they're just as valid as your guide appearing in front of you in full physical form. Not as spectacular, but the information transmitted can be just as relevant and life-changing.

Reason #3: We've never learnt the skills we need to communicate with our guides

Some people possess a natural gift for connecting with spirits. Everyone else needs to learn the basics. That doesn't mean they can never do it, but they have to learn *how*. Then practice. Even if you're born with this talent, you still need training. Super-talented soccer players train almost every single day. Just like them, if you want to succeed, you have to be willing to invest the time and effort. Regular meditation is a must, because it provides you with one-on-one time with your guides. Even if you don't see any progress right away, they'll be working hard to make the connection between you stronger every day. Other topics you need to learn about are psychic protection, raising your vibration, and the clairs, the inner senses we use to communicate with the spirit world. I'll cover all of these and more in the following chapters.

Reason #4: We doubt our experiences

Because mainstream culture regards spirit guides as figments of the imagination, we often doubt the experiences we have with them and therefore ourselves. We can combat this with regular practice. The more we communicate with our guides, the more confident we become that we aren't making things up. The more trust and confidence we build, the less time we spend doubting ourselves.

Another way to build confidence is to find like-minded people who share our interest in spirit guides. Hearing about their experiences, fears, and successes gives us the validation that we're not alone. It reminds us that millions of people all around the globe have similar spiritual experiences and that we aren't crazy. It's also useful to look at cultures that have a long history of spirit guide communication. No one in those cultures and spiritual traditions would doubt that spirit guides were real, and that we could talk to them and create alliances with them to create a better life for ourselves and others. Why should we doubt it?

No special gifts needed

Something else that might be holding us back is the idea that we need to be a psychic, shaman, witch, priest, medium, healer, or other professional spirit worker to connect with our spirit guides. That's not true at all. These are just the people we hear about in this context because they're the ones who have used their spirit guide connections to help others. An example is the famous 19th-century Vodou priestess Marie Laveau from New Orleans. She's even said to have saved several men from the gallows with her charms and spells. Other spirit workers have led their people into battle against enemies who have tried to oppress their community, like the Native American leader Sitting Bull, who had a vision that his people would win a major battle, which then happened in 1876. A very different and contemporary example would be Theresa Caputo, a medium from the USA. She's the star of her own TV show and teaches millions about life after death. But besides these famous examples, there are millions of unknown individuals around the globe who talk to their heavenly helpers daily. They're housewives, doctors, contractors, students, PR professionals, shopkeepers, farmers, lawyers, and more. They live their lives quietly and might not even tell their closest friends about their spiritual pursuits, but I know about them because I get emails from them every day in which they tell me their stories.

So, you don't need to be a spirit worker to communicate with your spirit guides, and you don't need any special abilities either. It's great to possess the ability to predict the future, heal through Reiki, read someone's aura, and so on. But you don't need spiritual gifts to receive guidance from your cosmic helpers. Or spiritual experiences. Have you had a near-death experience, traveled the astral world, or taken part in an ayahuasca ritual? If so, that's wonderful, but it's not a prerequisite for connecting with your guides. All you need is an open mind.

Unfortunately, few of us have been taught that approach, even though it's so important. As we saw earlier, we can get in our own way and not even realize that we're doing it. We block ourselves through limiting beliefs, early childhood conditioning, and unrealistic expectations. We close ourselves off without realizing it and therefore limit our potential. So let's first define what open-mindedness is before we look at *how* to achieve it. Keeping an open mind is the ability to be receptive to new ideas, concepts, and experiences without judging and rejecting them off the bat. Here are some tips to help you be open-minded as you read on:

Consider possibilities

If you read something that goes against what you believe to be true, consider the possibility there's more to reality than you assumed. Is it possible to expand your perspective to include both your pre-existing views and what you just read? Is there an overarching theme that incorporates both sets of information?

Don't be afraid to ask questions

If you're having a hard time wrapping your brain around a concept or a detail I introduce in this book, come and find me on social media. Let's have a conversation about it. It gives others the chance to chime in and allows all of us to walk away a little more enlightened than we were before.

Try everything at least once

This is something I learnt from my parents in the context of food, and I'll always be grateful for the lesson. If you assume that something I suggest you try won't work for you, or scares you, or seems too crazy to attempt, do it anyway, at least once. Maybe even twice to make sure you give it a fair chance. No risk, no gain.

If you get triggered or feel angry or frustrated, take time out

This can happen when you don't achieve the results you want right away. If you're a perfectionist like me, you'll know what I'm talking about. I've had students burst into tears because they didn't succeed in connecting with their guides after trying it for the very first time. I'm sure you're already sick of hearing it, but spirit guide communication takes practice. So, if you're feeling frustrated, be gentle and patient with yourself, take a break, and try again tomorrow.

Assume nothing

This is especially important for those of us who have spent years walking the spiritual path, as we sometimes fall into the trap of thinking we know everything already. Of course that's impossible. There's always a new skill to learn and a fresh perspective to consider. After every chapter of this book, ask yourself what was new to you and how you can incorporate it into your existing spiritual practice.

If you apply these principles, you won't just benefit from reading this book, you'll see your open mind having a positive effect on all areas of your life, from personal relationships to how you perform at work. Staying open-minded is also a great way to develop compassion, and we can never have enough of that in the world.

That said, here's one last tip:

Take what makes sense and leave the rest

If something doesn't work for you, discard it from your spiritual toolbox. You're the expert on your own life. You know best what serves you and what doesn't.

Remember, you're good enough already; you have everything you need to start this journey. Close your eyes for a moment. Take a deep breath and say out loud:

*I am willing and able to connect
with my spirit guides.*

I believe in you and so should you!

To support yourself on this journey, you can use the downloadable workbook (*see Bonuses, p.243*) that contains journaling prompts and serves as a place to reflect on what you read, take notes, and gather all the necessary information for your spirit guide ceremony in Chapter 12.

Now you're ready!

You now know that you're a lightworker who is part of a cosmic team and came here to make this world a better place for all beings. You've also learnt why you haven't succeeded in connecting with the spirit guide members of that team yet. And you understand that you don't need any special gifts or talents to communicate with your otherworldly team members, just an open mind. So now you're ready to dive in and get started.

~

Chapter 2

Spirit Guides 101

In this chapter I want to introduce you to the basic concepts and ideas you need to understand before getting to know your spirit guides better. Let's begin with a fundamental question:

What exactly is a spirit guide?

This question has been asked and answered many times. Here are some definitions from authors I admire:

'Spirit guides have once been physical beings.'
Sonia Choquette

*'Your spirit guides bring the wisdom
and perspective of many lifetimes.'*
James Van Praagh

*'We all have our own spirit guides.
We have guides that are ancestors
and deceased family members.'*

Gabby Bernstein

These important thought leaders have brought awareness to the topic of spirit guides and helped millions access their wisdom. And they're right: spirit guides *can* be ancestors or other deceased humans. In fact, the Western spirituality community often assumes that when help arrives from the spirit world, it almost always comes in the form of dead people. Many define a spirit as 'a human who has died.' This also implies that the spirit world is the equivalent of heaven, where dead people reside. These definitions are, often unknowingly, inspired by Spiritualism, a religious movement based on the belief that the spirits of the dead are wiser than the living and have the ability to communicate with and guide us. However, in other cultures and spiritual traditions, spirits can be many different non-physical beings and the spirit world is home to all of them, not just deceased humans. Thanks to authors like Kyle Gray and Diana Cooper, we now also know much more about angels, who also interact with and assist us. Besides that, the rise of Neo-Shamanism has introduced us to what are called 'power animals.' This is a concept based on the various animal spirits some Native American and many other shamanic cultures work with.

Other than those, we don't usually venture much further to look at the kind of beings other cultures, spiritual traditions, and individuals work with. What about the Dogon from Mali, whose spiritual support comes from beings in the star system Sirius? Or the 15 percent of Spirit Guide Society members, my community for lightworkers and spiritual seekers, who say their guide is a nature spirit? Or my client Sonya from Jordan, who came to a spirit guide reading accompanied by a goddess who had some life advice for her? In my experience as a spirit guide medium, spirit guides can take many forms. It's high time we look at this topic from a wider, more global, and more inclusive perspective. In doing so, not only do we honor cultures and wisdom beyond Western spirituality, we expand our own possibilities for connection.

Through the Internet and easier, faster ways to travel across the globe, our world is becoming more interconnected every day. In some of us, this creates anxiety, because we fear that our way of life is disappearing. So we build mental, emotional, and sometimes literal walls around ourselves. This also happens in the spiritual community. More often than not, we don't do this on purpose and don't mean to exclude anyone. But we do. By clinging to old concepts and refusing to update our knowledge of the spiritual realms, we alienate those who might need our help. We also turn away those who could guide us.

Another way the spiritual community isn't living up to its own standards is by seemingly embracing other cultures while in reality often perpetuating karmic ancestral behavioral patterns by taking from other spiritual traditions without offering respect. Giving something back often doesn't even occur to us. Since this is an important concept, we'll talk about it more throughout this book.

To make our spiritual communities more inclusive, we must start by redefining the core concepts we've worked with so far. We can then reconstruct our belief systems around these new definitions. Our own traditions need not disappear in the process. Instead, we can expand them and make them more open to the wisdom of others. This is a process and takes honest self-reflection. Even though I'm a product of multiple cultures and have spent many hours contemplating these topics, I still catch myself making mistakes. Don't be too hard on yourself. Take one step at a time. That's all it takes to create a more inclusive, egalitarian, and collaborative world.

My own guides inspired me to develop a new definition of spirit guides that I'd like to share with you here in the hope that it'll bring more awareness and inclusivity to the spiritual community:

Any being from the higher realms connected
to us in unconditional love who wants
to help us on our spiritual path or in
our day-to-day life is a spirit guide.

As you can see, this is a very wide definition and not limited to any specific belief system or geographic region.

In a second step, I'd like to present the seven different types or categories of spirit guide that we'll discuss in detail in Part II. The categorization of these seven types is an attempt to make it easier for you to identify and communicate with your personal spirit guides. It's not a dogmatic belief system. Over time, I might discover new types or learn more about existing ones. Spirituality isn't an exact science, and our interpretations can shift and morph, and should. None of us can grasp the full truth of what the spirit world is. All we can do is share our personal experiences with one another in order to grow together.

What my own spirit guide taught me

To go back to my personal experiences, after that first spirit guide showed up in my bedroom in the middle of the night, I tried to figure out what it all meant. I now knew he was my guide, but what did he want? And how could I connect and communicate with him again? It took me a long time to understand that the best way to talk to your guides depends on the type of guide you have. There are similarities and commonalities, but each type has its own communication preferences and even dislikes. Ancestor guides enjoy it when you create an altar for them, perform ceremonies, and bring some kind of offering. Nature spirits prefer it when you go outside, where they live, to connect with them. Deities demand respect and devotion and also like offerings. Angels respond well to prayer, meditation, and any activities that open the heart. I didn't know any of this at first, so I went through a lot of trial and error, which slowed the process.

Why did it take me so long to figure out that the guide I'd met was an ancestral guide? It was obvious right away that he was of indigenous descent and from South America, just like me. Still, my brain couldn't compute the information. I guess we all stand in our own way sometimes. It took me many years to put the puzzle pieces together because I wasn't yet used to the language the spirit world uses to communicate with humans (we'll talk about that more in Chapter 11). But at some point, I realized that he had to be my ancestor guide, because the messages I got were all related to my ancestry and the challenges and gifts that came with it.

More experiences followed and I had to develop a whole new mindset, a more expanded view of the world. What helped was doing massive amounts of research. This gave me the words to talk about my experiences and the knowledge to give them meaning.

Once I got used to the existence of non-physical beings, they started teaching me about the seven different types of spirit guide. This didn't happen all at once. As I explained earlier, over the next 15 years, various spirits showed up at random intervals, almost always in physical form. They rarely spoke, and I'd never see them again either. I had no clue what it all meant. But finally, I realized there was some logic to the otherworldly visits by different kinds of spirit: there were seven types of guide. Each had shown up at least once to introduce themselves to me.

Once I discovered there were seven types of spirit guide, things got a little easier. I researched how mediums, shamans, priests, witches, and other spirit workers connected with their respective guides, and over time things started falling into place. At the beginning of a new journey, though, everything seems confusing and overwhelming. And it's very hard to recognize the obvious when you've just had your first mind-blowing encounter with a spirit guide.

Now, on my free weekly live show I get asked a lot of questions. Some answers are obvious to me, and I'm glad I can help clarify things for people. One question I get asked a lot is: 'What does see my dead grandmother/an angel/an elf/etc. mean?' The answer is simple. It's a wake-up call. The spirit world is trying to get your attention. Spirits are ready to work with you.

Once I realized I was dealing with an ancestor guide, I signed up for an ayahuasca ritual with a Colombian shaman. Not because it was the newest spiritual fad. I did it because I found out this was one way my indigenous ancestors connected with the spirit world. Many people do ayahuasca ceremonies because they want spectacular visions and otherworldly experiences, but I'd done my research and knew that the healing these ceremonies provided was their main benefit, not the fireworks that sometimes came with them. I'm telling you this because there's an important lesson to learn here: only take ayahuasca if you feel really called to do so. It's not for everyone. Do your research, only work with authentic and experienced facilitators, make sure you're in a safe environment, and keep your expectations in check! During the ritual, I didn't see my ancestor guide in physical form again, but I sensed my ancestors as a group energy that communicated with me through feelings. The love, support, and inclusion I felt healed a part of my heart that had been deeply wounded. In the long run this enabled me to also fully cherish the love that already existed in my life, especially that of my parents.

After that first time taking part in this kind of ceremony, I realized a huge shift had taken place inside me. I felt more grounded, more anchored, and I knew what the next step would be on my journey to discovering and living my purpose.

This illustrates perfectly that once you find out what type of guide you have, you can use the knowledge that others have already gathered about connecting with them and apply it for yourself. You don't want to appropriate other people's culture or spiritual tradition, but you can gather inspiration from them. To stay with the ancestor example, this book will provide you with some ideas about how others go about connecting with their ancestors. Then you can determine what makes sense for you to try out and what doesn't. You don't want to chant in a language you don't even understand, but maybe you can come up with your own affirmations and chant those. Or, instead of using sage, which is traditionally used by some Native American cultures for cleansing an area before an ancestor ceremony, you could look into what herbs or incenses are used by local spiritual traditions and use those to cleanse the room. Always be mindful and respectful toward the cultures that teach you valuable lessons and give back wherever possible.

Do your own research, too. If your ancestors are from India, for example, dig into your own culture and find out what your grandmothers and grandfathers did to talk to the deceased. Maybe your Turkish great-grandmother read the coffee grounds deposited at the bottom of her cup to see what the future would bring, so it might be worth learning more about that way of receiving information from the spirit world. Or maybe your Senegalese father's lineage always maintained a family altar. To whom was that altar dedicated? Are there sacred objects that have been passed down from generation to generation? It's also worth enquiring about your 'crazy' Aunt Mabel. Ask your family members about her. What's her story? Why do people think she's a bit cuckoo?

It's amazing how often these stigmatized relatives are the ones who speak to elves, angels, or the dead. You might even heal some family karma by being the first to take them seriously.

Communication with our guides doesn't always happen through direct contact either, but more often through subtle inspiration while we're doing the spiritual grunt work like research and daily mindfulness. Knowing which type of guides you have helps you to find out how to make it easy for them to reach you and inspire you daily.

The seven types of spirit guide

Now that you know what a spirit guide is, let's take a closer look at the seven different types of guide. As stated earlier, all spirit guides are from the higher realms, connected to us through unconditional love, and they want to help us on our spiritual path. However, they come from different places and dimensions of the Universe. They possess different characteristics and bring distinctive gifts and challenges for those working with them. The different types can be more or less common in certain cultures and spiritual traditions, they enjoy distinct ways of connecting with humans, and are diverse in many other ways. We'll devote a whole chapter to each one of them. For now, let me give you a quick overview:

Deities

There are gods and goddesses in many cultures and spiritual traditions. Some see them as omnipotent, eternal, and the creators of the Universe. Others perceive them as powers of nature, like the wind, lightning, or the sea. Another way to define them is as ancestors who have been moved up the ranks for their heroic deeds or moral integrity. Last, they can be different representations, aspects, or paths of one supreme being. Most times, they possess human-like personalities and their own agendas and desires. They demand respect and devotion and in exchange make powerful allies.

Ancestors

Ancestors are those who lived before us and are no longer with us in our physical dimension. This includes your parents, grandparents, and other people you knew in this lifetime. However, it also includes family members who lived hundreds or even thousands of years ago and are long forgotten by history.

In a broader sense, your ancestors are also those who made you the person you are today, on all levels of life. You can belong to lineages that go beyond genetics. They're often based on vocation, culture, and spirituality.

Ascended masters

Ascended masters are human beings who once lived on Earth and gained the wisdom and mastery needed to reach enlightenment. They attained such a high spiritual awareness that they ascended. This means they're free from karma, have merged with their higher selves, and need not reincarnate anymore. Instead, they reside in the sixth dimension or above and assist us from there. They were often masters of their own spiritual traditions when they were on Earth, and they still seek the highest good for humanity and promote peace and compassion.

Nature spirits

Nature spirits have been known throughout history and across the globe. Each culture and spiritual tradition distinguishes different types and has its own names for them. Most acknowledge those connected to the elements: the spirits of water, air, earth, and fire. Besides these, there are nature spirits who inhabit certain mountains, trees, rivers, or other natural features that are important or stand out to the local human community. Mother Earth herself is also widely recognized as a sentient being in her own right.

Animal guides

Another type of spirit guide known by people around the world is the animal spirit. It's important to acknowledge the different names and definitions used. Some traditions call these guides the Mothers, Fathers, Lords, or Masters of a specific animal species, like the Mother of Fish or the Master of Jaguars. Others work with totem animals, the spirit of an animal related to a group of people like a family, clan, or lineage. We also have 'familiars,' a term from European medieval folklore that describes the animal spirits who assist witches practicing their magic, and the power animals of the Neo-Shamanic tradition.

Star beings

The broad definition of star beings is that they're any kind of life-form that's *not* native to Earth. There are an infinite variety of life-forms present in our Universe and beyond. Some have a physical body, others don't. Some are humanoid, others aren't. There are also the stars themselves. Since every human, animal, plant, and rock has its own spirit, as does Mother Earth herself, so does every star and every star system, galaxy, nebula, etc. They're all sentient and can connect with us.

Angels

The word 'angel' comes from the Greek *aggelos*, which means 'messenger.' This makes sense, since angels act as intermediaries between us and the Divine. Some people are convinced that angels have never lived as humans on Earth, but others state that they can incarnate and have done so for millennia. The Sumerians, Egyptians, ancient Greeks, and Romans certainly mention them in their texts. Most famous among the angels are the archangels: Michael, the protector; Raphael, the healer; Gabriel, the nurturer; Zadkiel, the transformer; Uriel, the light-bringer; and Metatron, the celestial scribe.

What about God?

I sometimes get asked why we're talking to guides when we could talk to God instead. This is a question mostly asked by people with a religious background. My answer is that we can talk to God *and* to spirit guides! Who says we have to choose? I see God/the

Universe/the Creator/Spirit/etc. as the totality of everything that exists, seen or unseen. Therefore, spirit guides, like all other beings, including ourselves, are part of God, and there's nothing wrong with communicating with them. In fact, these evolved beings act as God's ambassadors.

The benefits of working with spirit guides

As you've seen by now, I gained a lot from working with my personal spirit guides. I connected with my ancestors on a spiritual level, which gave me a sense of grounding; I developed my spiritual abilities, found my purpose in connecting people with their own cosmic helpers, and learnt to trust myself and the Universe more. You can receive the same kind of benefits if you learn how to communicate with your guides. I'll showcase seven benefits here, but there are many more for you to discover!

Alignment with the higher self

To access our own inner wisdom, strength, and courage, we need to align our physical, incarnated self with our spiritual self, also known as the higher self. Once they merge and there's no more separation between the two, they can work together. In these moments, we flow in harmony with life. Our spirit guides can help us remove the blocks and heal the rifts that keep our two selves from working together as one. This is a gradual process. Like developing any new skill, it takes time, but our guides are eager to support us along the way.

Getting rid of ego blocks

We all need our ego. If we didn't have it, we couldn't survive in our physical reality. It's important that part of us watches out for danger and makes sure all our physical needs are met. However, if our ego takes over and tries to run the show, it can block our spiritual development. We don't want that to happen and our guides don't want that either. So they guide us into life situations that help us resolve the ego blocks that stand in our way. We can then reach a state of balance and serve as a bridge between worlds, which facilitates communication.

Development of spiritual gifts

We're all psychic! Every one of us can receive information through our intuition. In Western society, this skill often stays underdeveloped because we perceive it to be of little value compared to the rational mind. However, it's like a muscle that gets stronger through regular training, and we can develop it enough to communicate with our spirit guides and pick up other information too.

A better sense of how to serve

After developing our spiritual gifts, we'll feel more confident about serving others and the world at large. We know we have unique skills that can help our fellow humans. How can we use them right now in our everyday life to help others in ways big and small? Developing a mindset of service is a stepping stone to discovering our life purpose. And then...

Naturally living our life purpose

Finding their purpose is a wish high on the list of many spiritual people. They sense a little voice deep inside their heart calling them to be of service to the world. So many of us sense this, but don't know how to serve and spend years wondering while we make our money in a job that doesn't fulfill us. But even if you think you don't know what your purpose is, your soul and your spirit guides know very well. Let them assist you in discovering what you came here to do.

Increased trust in the Universe and ourselves

Another benefit of working with our heavenly helpers is that we trust the Universe and ourselves more. This happens when we realize that our spirit guides have always been talking to us, it's just that our rational mind has ignored their messages, for reasons we discussed earlier. To do so, we've had to reject our intuition, which has resulted in distrusting ourselves and the Universe. Once we learn to listen to our intuition again, it's easier to trust ourselves again. We also realize that the Universe is working with us, not against us.

General mentorship and guidance

The benefits listed previously are just a selection of what you can expect from working with spirit guides. You can expect a lot more. As long as you align your goals and desires with the highest good of all, your guides are happy to assist you in achieving and reaching them. You can see them as your spiritual mentors in life. This doesn't mean they'll solve all your problems for you. You came here to experience life, not to get through it as quickly as possible using a cheat sheet like you can in a video game. It does mean that you're never alone and support is always nearby. How amazing is that?

~

Next, we'll look at the dangers of working with spirit guides. Not that your guides would ever harm or hurt you. The dangers stem from your own ego and its reaction to the expanded worldview, increased personal power, and exposure to new spiritual truths that come from working with spirit guides. I don't mean to scare you, but, as with everything in life, there are risks. And it's better to know what *not* to do before you begin.

The dangers of working with spirit guides

Some people don't believe there are risks involved when connecting with the spirit world. They've either never considered the question because to them it's all 'love and light' or they think there are no negative entities residing there. I don't agree. Even though I've never suffered negative consequences from embarking on my spiritual journey, I've observed them in others and heard too many accounts that I can't dismiss. Almost every single culture and spiritual tradition has standard procedures to protect people from the negative effects of spirit communication. There's a reason for that. However, the better you prepare, the less likely you are to run into any problems. So let's address the four issues that might show up when you attempt to connect with your spirit guides.

In reality, the bigger danger is your own ego which, if unchecked, might cause harm to yourself and/or others. Knowledge is power and can prevent 99 percent of the dangers involved, so read the following section carefully.

Evil spirits

Do they exist? Depending on your personal spiritual tradition or cultural heritage, your answer will be different. My stance is that, just like humans, there are friendly spirits and not so friendly spirits. Even if I wouldn't classify the vast majority of the latter as evil, they might have a different agenda than you and not care about your wellbeing. This means to assume that all spirits have your best interests at heart is, in my opinion, naïve. In our physical reality, we don't hang out in bad neighborhoods to make new friends and don't invite random strangers into our house. The same rules apply when working with the spirit world. You want to use discernment and build trust. Take things slowly. Don't rush into a relationship with a potential spirit guide. Get to know them first. That said, please note that there's a difference between random spirits and spirit guides. Not all spirits are benevolent and here to help you. But, by definition, all spirit guides are! Remember, only those from the higher realms who are connected to us in unconditional love can become our spirit guides. I'll teach you how to make sure no unwanted visitors come along for the ride in the last part of this book, before you get to meet your own guide via a ceremony.

A guru complex

Another challenge you might encounter on your spirit guide journey is ego inflation, which sometimes manifests as a guru complex. In a severe case, someone might think they're the actual Second Coming of Christ or another religious figure, about to save the world, and expect everyone around them to bow down and worship them. We've all heard of the cult leaders who abuse their followers on an emotional, mental, and even sexual level. They often legitimize their actions by claiming they're following the directions of a spirit guide. In reality, it's just their ego leading them astray. To avoid this danger, always stay humble and realize that yes, you're special and unique, but so is everyone else. Your guides would never encourage you to put yourself above others.

Cultural appropriation

Besides physical and intellectual property, there's also spiritual property. Since we all know it's not okay to steal someone else's car or song lyrics, we should also realize that stealing someone's spiritual heritage is equally unjust. It's okay to be inspired by others, but just taking the spiritual knowledge they've gained over hundreds or even thousands of years won't serve you. First, there's the very real possibility that people suffered and died to protect their cultural heritage during times of colonization and occupation. It's disrespectful to just take what we want and not respect their ownership. Second, their practices won't work for you, because without cultural understanding, they lose their meaning. Here's what to do instead: try to understand why, for example, a certain culture offers corn beer to their spirit guides and then find a local alternative or find a practice from your own culture that yields the same results. Also, consider giving back to your teachers, even if you don't know them in real life and have only read about their practices in a book or online. If their knowledge helps you, consider donating to a cause that supports them in exchange (examples: Survival International, Cultural Survival, Amazon Conservation Team).

Spiritual bypassing

Using spirituality to avoid emotional and psychological issues is another risk you face when working with spirit guides. Again, it's your ego at work, looking for an excuse to bypass reality. If you find yourself spending too much time in spiritual retreats and too much money on courses and workshops, stop and examine why. Are you running away from certain problems in your daily life?

Another way spiritual bypassing shows up is if you suppress unpleasant emotions in the name of a spiritual ideal. Life is hard and it can seem easier to close our eyes to that harsh truth. But any spiritual behavior that shields us from unresolved issues is unhealthy. If you find this happening, examine the motivations behind it and, if necessary, get help from a therapist.

Now that you know what a spirit guide is, which types of guide exist, and what the benefits and dangers of working with them are, it's time to take the quiz. Are you ready to find out which of the seven types of spirit guide you have?

~

CHAPTER 3

The Quiz: Which Types of Spirit Guide Do You Have?

My career as a spirit guide medium started with taking a nap. It was the summer of 2016 and I was living in Barcelona, Spain. I was running a business helping artists sell their creative work online, but felt unmotivated and unfulfilled. Thankfully, I knew myself well enough to realize that I'd entered a transitional phase in my life and that what I needed was lots of rest, patience, and self-care. I made sure to listen to my intuition and my guides instead of my inner critic, who just kept telling me what I *should* be doing – mainly keeping busy and ignoring my intuition.

It wasn't the first time I'd found myself in a situation like this and I knew things would work out eventually. Still, one afternoon I was feeling particularly frustrated and lost. I decided to lie down for a bit in the hope that I'd feel better afterward. When I woke up from that nap, my mind still unfocused and the world around me blurry, I felt my crown chakra open up and information rush into me like a wave. I'd received a major download that would alter the course of my life forever. I'd been asked by the spirit world to start doing spirit guide readings for paying clients.

Collaborating with Spirit

Amazingly, the download also provided me with a complete marketing plan, including the idea for the shorter web version of the quiz presented in this chapter. However, I didn't receive any guidance on the actual questions to include in it, so I had to do some serious research into how quizzes were created and then use my own experiences with spirit guides to devise the questions.

This goes to show that working with Spirit doesn't mean that everything is presented on a silver platter. It's always a collaboration – our guides do their part and we have to do ours. In my case, they delivered the spark of inspiration and guidance for marketing, and I had to grab my laptop, teach myself how to create a quiz, and then actually put it online. This collaboration led me to start a new chapter in my life – and eventually write this book!

Occasionally this need for collaboration prevents us from understanding when our spirit guides are communicating with us. In many cases, they've already given us their advice and are just waiting for us to take the human steps involved to make things happen! It's only when we've done our part that they'll guide us further along our path.

So, when you get a message from your guide, listen closely – and then be ready to follow up on their advice on the physical plane. Be willing to take a step on your own and then tune back in for a clue as to where to go from there. Yes, there's a time for meditation and prayer, but there's also a time for action.

After receiving this powerful message from my guides, I took action and developed a version of the following quiz based on my observations of people, their guides, and how they work together to do incredible things.

I knew from my own experiences that once I'd created the online quiz, more information would be revealed to me that would eventually lead me to a happier and more fulfilled life. And I wasn't wrong.

∾ THE SPIRIT GUIDE QUIZ ∾

I've made this quiz as straightforward as possible. It consists of 25 questions, each with seven possible answers. Go through the questions one by one and choose the answer that comes closest to your own opinion, experience, or thoughts on the matter. Don't skip any questions and only choose one answer each time. Lastly, don't overthink things – let your intuition guide you.

You can take an online version if you prefer (*see Bonuses, p.243*).

Okay? Now, let's get started. Do you want to know which of the seven types of cosmic helper are working with you right now?

1. **When you were young, what were your favorite bedtime stories, movies, and books about?**

   A. Heroes with superpowers

   G. Heavenly helpers coming to the rescue

   E. Animals

   F. Space or life on other planets

   D. Nature and wilderness adventures

   B. Ghosts or the past – stories your grandparents would tell you

   C. Monks, nuns, saints, or other spiritually minded people

2. **What do you most like to do in your free time?**

   A. Create things

   E. Volunteer at the local animal shelter

   G. Support others with whatever they need

   C. Meditate

   B. Spend time with my family

   F. Anything related to my computer, social media, or the Internet

   D. Hike and spend time in nature

3. **What kind of spiritual healing have you done or would you like to do?**

   A. A ceremony in a pyramid

   G. Twin-flame karma release

   D. An ayahuasca ceremony

   E. Swimming with dolphins

   F. A Reiki session

   B. Ancestral healing

   C. A silent meditation retreat

4. **How do you experience your intuition?**

   D. In my gut or as a physical sensation

   G. As an emotion or feeling in my heart area

   F. As a sudden insight or lightbulb moment

   A. As a request or command

   E. As an unconscious instinct

   C. As advice or a lesson

   B. On a very deep and cellular level

5. **What superpower would you like to have?**

   F. Telepathy

   E. Shapeshifting

   D. Instant manifestation

   G. Healing powers

B. Speaking to the dead

C. Infinite wisdom and knowledge

A. Immortality

6. **What's the craziest spiritual experience you've ever had (or would like to have)?**

D. I was visited by an elf, gnome, or mermaid

B. I saw a ghost

G. I was overcome by love and gratitude and surrounded by a white light and sparkles

C. I reached an enlightened state while meditating

E. I felt that I'd transformed into an animal

F. I had an encounter with an alien or UFO

A. I was crowned as a king/queen or put in another important leadership position

7. **What is your favorite food?**

G. Dessert and sweets

A. A big banquet with lots of choices

C. A simple but nourishing meal

D. Fruits and vegetables

E. Meat

B. Our favorite family recipe

F. I eat because I have to, not for pleasure

8. **What would you like your spirit guides to help you with?**

    G. Helping others in some capacity

    A. Becoming more powerful

    F. Understanding and healing my feelings of not belonging on this planet

    D. Saving the planet from destruction

    E. Fighting for animal rights

    B. Improving family relationships

    C. Reaching enlightenment

9. **What kind of imaginary friend did you have or would you have liked as a child?**

    E. A tiger, wolf, or dragon

    G. An angel

    B. My deceased grandmother or grandfather

    D. A fairy, mermaid, gnome, or an elf

    A. A god or goddess

    F. A visitor from another planet

    C. A wise, patient, and compassionate teacher

10. **Where would you like to live?**

    A. In a castle

    D. In a house in the countryside

    F. In a futuristic house with all the newest technology

E. On a farm

C. In a monastery or ashram

B. In a house that's belonged to my family for generations

G. In a home with white minimalist interior design and a calm, peaceful atmosphere

11. **As a kid, what did you think you wanted to be when you grew up?**

G. A nurse, teacher, or other person who helped others

F. A scientist or an astronaut

E. A veterinarian or other person who worked with animals

D. A park ranger, environmentalist, or gardener

A. Famous!

C. A monk or nun

B. Just like a favorite family member

12. **Which of the below best describes the type of upbringing you had?**

A. Strict but fair

C. My parents always trusted me to make wise decisions for myself

F. I felt like a bit of an outsider in my own family

G. Even as a child I had to take care of others (such as parents or siblings)

B. At least one of my family members suffered from abuse or addiction

D. I was encouraged to spend as much time outdoors as possible

E. I learnt to be competitive early on

13. **If you had the chance to do one of the things listed below, which would it be?**

E. To make sure that humans respect the rights of the other living beings on Earth

A. To bring the leaders of the world together to create world peace

C. To plant the ability to make wise decisions in everyone's heart

G. To heal all the sick and feed all the hungry

D. To clean up the environment

B. To ensure that future generations don't make the same mistakes we did

F. To create technology that gives everyone the freedom to pursue their dreams

14. **What is your favorite way to connect with the Divine?**

D. Out in nature

E. Through physical activity

A. With a joyous celebration

F. In community

B. Using ritual or ceremony

C. Journaling

G. Prayer

15. **What do you struggle with the most?**

    A. Handling my responsibilities

    B. Family relationships

    D. Self-discipline

    F. Expressing emotions

    C. Being too verbose

    G. Self-worth

    E. Anger issues

16. **Where would you prefer to go on vacation?**

    B. The Great Wall of China, the Egyptian Pyramids, or the Colosseum in Rome

    F. A hacker camp, a cryptocurrency convention, or Burning Man

    D. Hiking in the Grand Canyon, skiing in the Alps, or camping at the beach

    C. A writing retreat, the Buddhist temples of Thailand, or a yoga retreat in India

    G. A luxurious spa, a resort in the Bahamas, or a shopping trip to New York City

A. A rented castle with a butler, Richard Branson's Necker Island, or Balmoral, the summer residence of the Queen of England

E. A safari, a sports hotel, or a survival camp

17. **How do you spend your weekends?**

D. Having a good time with my friends

A. Pampering myself

G. Taking care of everyone else and then relaxing with a glass of wine in the evenings

C. Reading

F. Working on my computer

E. Exercising at the gym

B. Spending quality time with my family

18. **What cause would you donate money to?**

C. An initiative to record the oral wisdom of the indigenous peoples of the world

E. A rescue shelter for traumatized animals

F. A research program to find life on other planets

D. A rainforest conservation organization

G. An orphanage

A. A leadership program for outstanding youth from underprivileged communities around the world

B. An archeological expedition to find the remnants of Atlantis and Lemuria

19. **Which of the following describes the past life you'd most like to have had?**

    C. A nun or monk in Tibet

    G. The head of a charity helping street kids in Victorian England

    F. The creator of an important invention that changed humanity forever

    A. A king or queen

    D. A traditional healer who worked with plants

    B. A member of an ancient shamanic tribe

    E. A lion

20. **How would you like to celebrate your next birthday?**

    A. A big party. Everyone is invited!

    G. A fundraiser for my favorite charity

    B. Surrounded by my dearest family members and friends

    F. An event with a live stream to include all the friends I've made online

    C. Just me and a book

    D. A beach gathering

    E. A fun day engaged in my favorite physical activities

21. **If you only had one year to live, how would you spend it?**

    F. Developing an Artificial Intelligence that lets me communicate from the other side when I'm gone

    B. Making sure my loved ones know how much I appreciate them

    A. Creating a legacy I can be remembered by

    C. Preparing for the spiritual transformation that death brings

    E. Living quietly in the country with all of my pets

    G. Making sure that everyone will be taken care of after I've passed away

    D. On a tour of the most beautiful places on Earth

22. **How do you sabotage yourself?**

    D. I tend to distrust other humans

    B. I have a hard time trying new things

    G. I have addictive tendencies

    C. I can be a bit of a know-it-all

    E. I can be too impulsive

    A. I've been told that I'm bossy

    F. I don't always deal well with emotions

23. **What do you admire most in others?**

    A. Power

    C. Wisdom

E. Decisiveness

G. Empathy

F. Intelligence

D. Creativity

B. Rootedness

24. **What kind of celebrities do you admire?**

B. Historic figures

F. Scientists

D. Environmentalists

A. Leaders

G. Philanthropists

C. Spiritual teachers

E. Sports professionals

25. **Which of these activities relaxes you most?**

F. Engaging in my favorite hobby

D. Gardening

G. Having a glass of wine

B. Spending time with my loved ones

E. Moving my body

A. Knowing that someone else is in charge, for now

C. Meditation

PROCESSING YOUR RESULTS

Once you've answered all the questions, go over them again and count how many of the answers you ticked for each type of spirit guide, as follows:

A	Deities
B	Ancestors
C	Ascended masters
D	Nature spirits
E	Animal guides
F	Star beings
G	Angels

Once you identify the three types of spirit guide you scored highest for, flip to their corresponding chapters to learn more about each unique guide. In doing this you'll begin to form a deep understanding of the guides around you. If you score high in only one or two categories and almost the same in the others, then let your intuition guide you and read the chapters that call to you or interest you most. Trust that this will be exactly right for you.

If you still feel confused, you can't go wrong by reading Chapter 5, on ancestor guides. We all have these, and many spiritual traditions require spirit workers in training to work with the ancestors first.

It's important to remember that you have a whole team of guides. So, once you've identified the ones that are in strongest alignment with you, move on to read the rest of the chapters. Then listen to your intuition and tune in to the other cues around you. Be alert for messages and signals from your other guides and eventually they'll reveal themselves to you one by one.

How do you know when you've identified your entire team? You don't. Even though you have a core team that stays with you your entire life, other guides come and go, depending on your current life circumstances and where you are on your spiritual journey.

~

PART II

The
Seven Types
of Spirit
Guide

Chapter 4

DEITIES

I can trace my connection to one of my deity guides all the way back to 23 December 1999, when I was still a student in Germany. I was on a train, going to visit my parents in Belgium for Christmas. A few days before, my friend Bianca had shown me a little book called *Secrets of the Cube: The Ancient Visualization Game That Reveals Your True Self* by Annie Gottlieb. Back then, I was still very much trying to figure out who I was and what I wanted to do with my future, so the book piqued my interest. Once settled into my seat on the train, with the winter landscape flashing past my window, I opened the book and began reading.

First, the author asked me to visualize a desert. I closed my eyes and allowed my imagination to conjure up beautiful white sand dunes with majestic mountains in the background. Next, she guided me to add a cube. I took a breath and in my mind's eye saw a tiny square lumber hut in the distance. The air around me on the train suddenly became thicker, my skin started tingling, and my crown chakra opened up. I then felt myself fall into a very light trance that enabled the visualization to morph into a vision. I no longer felt as if I was creating the images I saw; instead, they were being given to me. I put the book down on my lap and let myself be pulled into the desert, where the sun was shining brightly, the air was shimmering with heat, and everything was quiet. My consciousness floated toward the little house in the distance. It couldn't have contained more than one small room. As I got closer, I saw that it was hovering above the sand, and had a window and a door in the front-facing wall. The door was open and a woman was standing in the doorway.

Right away I knew this woman. I recognized her energy immediately, even though I couldn't remember ever having seen her before. My heart chakra opened and a flood of love entered my heart. She smiled and my spirit felt embraced and welcomed. I was home. Tears started streaming down my face. My human self had no idea what was happening, but my higher self knew that something significant had just occurred. I kept my eyes closed until the vision slowly disintegrated like wisps of mist, my consciousness settled back into my body, and my senses became aware of the other passengers on the train. Even though I didn't realize it then, looking back I now know that this was the first time that Yemaya, the goddess of the sea in the West African Yoruba tradition, connected with me.

It took many similar experiences before I connected the dots and realized that Yemaya was trying to communicate with me. She'd used my visualization exercise to make the first contact, even if that meant exchanging her usual watery home for the desert. She's never appeared to me physically, like many of the other

56

beings I've met over the years. Instead, my relationship with her developed gradually and slowly. This is a big part of how spirit communication works; it's all about setting aside expectations and accepting that talking to spirits requires learning a whole new language, and this takes time.

Yemaya wasn't an immediately obvious guide for me, since I've never been officially initiated into one of the African diaspora religions (and, therefore, don't profess to speak for them, but trust my own experiences). However, once she started making contact, I reflected deeply on her presence and the connection began to make sense. I'm a Virgo with a Pisces ascendant (half-woman, half-fish), my birth mother's name is Marina (which means 'from the sea'), people love gifting me jewelry (one of the offerings often made to Yemaya), and I love taking long baths. Furthermore, during ayahuasca ceremonies I always have visions of swimming with mermaids. These are all little details of my life that individually don't feel very significant, but when taken together as a whole make it clear to me that Yemaya, the mother of fish, is one of my spirit companions, and why.

Since that first contact, she's guided me in my spiritual development in the unique way of a deity. She's led me along a path of experiences that have boosted my sense of self-worth and eventually helped me become a wayshower to those who want to learn more about their own spirit guides. Perhaps surprisingly, she's also guiding me in building my business. At first you might not expect the mother of fish to be a genius in online marketing. But in the Yoruba Orisha traditions, one of her many names is Yemaya Mayelewo, and in this form she's said to be good with money and business. I can definitely attest to that, since she makes my skin tingle every time a beneficial business opportunity comes along and she regularly leads me to clients and teachers who also turn out to be connected to her!

What exactly are deities?

When it comes to deities, otherwise known as gods and goddesses, there's no consensus on what they are. In the monotheistic religions like Christianity, Judaism, and Islam, there's only one god, who is viewed as omnipotent, eternal, and the creator of the Universe. The belief in one all-powerful god who intervenes in the world stems from the late Bronze Age and was (and often still is) considered to be the only *real* religion by Western theologians. Of course, that's not true.

In polytheism, which is found in ancient Greece, and in Shinto, Santeria, and various Neo-Pagan faiths, deities frequently have two different origins: they can be powers of nature, like the wind, lightning, or the sea, or ancestors who have been moved up the ranks in acknowledgement of their heroic deeds or moral integrity. Both deified powers of nature and evolved ancestors are generally portrayed with human-like personalities, complete with positive and negative emotions. Each has their own agenda, and goals they try to reach with the help of their devotees. Some of these goals might be the spiritual elevation of humankind, the preservation of a culture and its traditions, keeping the universal balance, or simply experiencing the joys and pleasures of physical life through the Earthly senses of an incarnated soul.

Then there's henotheism, which states that all gods and goddesses are different representations, aspects, or paths of one supreme being. This belief is found in Zoroastrianism, Hinduism, and in some ways the Church of Jesus Christ of Latter-day Saints (Mormonism).

If any of these definitions and schools of thought are new to you, don't worry, you don't have to memorize them. What is important is to reflect on your own stance and what you believe in. You don't have to believe what your parents told you or what the religion you grew up with proclaims to be true. There are many spiritual paths available to you. Spirituality is a topic that has no clear-cut answers and, in the end, comes down to the subjective reality experienced by individuals. In fact, this is the whole point of this book! I want you to experience your spirit guides for yourself without anyone telling you what you should believe. I will say, though, that looking at the deities and spiritual beliefs of other cultures, traditions, and individuals throughout history can be very helpful as you start your own explorations. These open your mind in a way that can be hard to do on your own.

For now, take a moment, close your eyes, and ask yourself what the idea of deity looks and feels like to you. This by itself can be a major clue in finding out which deity you're working with. Sit with your thoughts for a moment. Does 'deity' feel male or female? Far away or close by? Authoritative or wise and loving? Powerful or gentle? Large or small?

In order to define the term 'deity' for the purpose of this book, and to keep that definition as open and inclusive as possible, we'll look to pantheism, yet another way to classify religions by how they perceive deity. Pantheism assumes that all of existence is part of one unifying supreme force and that nothing exists separately from this force, whether that's called God/Goddess, the Universe, All That Is, Source, Spirit, or anything else. We'll also acknowledge a multitude of gods and goddesses who exist independently of each other, have almost human-like personalities, and deliberately seek out contact with us – like my guide, the goddess Yemaya. These are the deities with whom we can have a deep personal relationship. They're supreme beings with supernatural powers and an often heroic attitude. They can raise our consciousness to a higher level and help us reach our goals in the physical world. How amazing is that?

Guide characteristics

Even though gods and goddesses may possess widely varying personality traits, from the frantic and furious nature of Odin to the graceful and forgiving guidance of Lakshmi, they have a lot in common, and there are certain characteristics that set them apart as a group. There are three main traits that distinguish them from the other types of spirit guide. Understanding these unique traits will help you identify and connect with the god or goddess personally guiding you.

Authoritative

The energy of deities generally feels regal and authoritative. This is because they reside on a higher plane, meaning they're on a different energy frequency where they have a more elevated view of existence. This is like comparing someone who is crossing a road and can only see what's going on around them to someone sitting on a rooftop terrace who can observe the pedestrian in the street, the high-rise behind them, and the dog playing with a toy in the yard across the street. Like the rooftop observer, deities simply observe a bigger slice of reality. This gives them a certain power (and responsibility) that we don't possess on our own.

Sometimes this power can spark an instinctively fearful reaction when we first meet a deity guide. Be aware that if you feel this, it doesn't mean that you're in contact with a negative or even evil entity, it just means that a part of you recognizes you're in the presence of a magnificent spirit with higher power. This is why I like to characterize this guide group as 'authoritative' – our intuition will sense their authority right away, and this is one meaningful way to recognize their presence. When I meditate and connect with Yemaya by blending my energy with hers, I can feel when she arrives because I automatically sit up straighter and see the world as if from a throne. Religious, cultural, and political leaders from around the world often base their authority on a calling from or connection with a deity. They're that powerful.

Demanding devotion

The second distinctive characteristic of deities is closely connected to their authoritative nature, and this is the fact that they ask for our loyalty and devotion. My guide Yemaya, for example, loves it when I do research into her and the spiritual lineages serving her.

Even though that might not be a traditional way to worship her, she seems to enjoy the fact that I devote my time to her in this way.

Over the years, one way that we've expressed our devotion to deities has been by building beautiful and elaborate temples to them. Historically, these endeavors have required massive amounts of time, energy, and manpower. The hope has been that devoting so much time and effort into the relationship with the gods will translate into greater blessings and gifts for the spiritual community.

However, once you commune with a deity, remember that the highest form of devotion is to understand the duty, responsibility, and purpose that deity has in regard to the rest of the Universe. Then bring yourself into alignment with that purpose. Deity guides will encourage you to surrender your ego in favor of a life devoted to working for a higher good. One way I do this is by helping Yemaya to preserve the ancient tradition of spirit communication in a fresh way that applies to modern-day people. That takes a lot of time and energy, but also makes my life richer and more interesting.

Involved in human affairs

The last characteristic of deities to be aware of is their frequent interference in human matters. Ancestors (*see Chapter 5*) are also closely entwined with human lives, but on a smaller scale, because they're focused on the goals of a certain lineage or cultural group. Gods and goddesses, on the other hand, are known to have initiated large-scale events with a big impact on the whole of humanity. These range from tragedies like wars, famines, and natural disasters to the seemingly more miraculous such as the introduction of new foods, the inspiration of great works of art, and the creation of empires.

This intimate involvement with human matters can also be expressed on a personal level. When working with a deity, you may feel that you're regularly asked to do certain things. For instance, Yemaya has invited me to actively seek out other spirit workers connected to her and learn from them. This personal involvement only happens when it serves a higher purpose, with an end goal in mind, and you can trust that if you follow through, your efforts will have a positive impact on your life.

Gifts

The gifts that come from a close bond with deities are numerous. Many stories have been passed down from generation to generation of heroes, kings, and commoners who were given a superpower or two by a god or goddess. Superhuman strength, the ability to fly, and the capacity to transform into an animal are just a few classic examples. But let's focus on the three gifts from deity guides that are most likely to have a lasting and positive effect on your life.

Leadership skills

As mentioned earlier, many religious and secular leaders have based their authority on an affiliation with a deity – and we all know that a lot of abuse has taken place in the name of the gods when it was really the ego that reigned. But why is it that people in leadership positions seem to have a bond with gods?

For one, a deity will usually work with individuals who already show the propensity to become great leaders in their respective communities (even if they don't recognize that themselves). Secondly, the deity connection itself inspires people to take responsibility for their own lives and those of their fellow humans instead of just letting their circumstances dictate their destiny, thus shaping them into leaders.

So, a deity guide will help shift your perspective from one dominated by the ego to one motivated by a bigger purpose and will encourage you to be the leader you were meant to be. This doesn't mean that all of a sudden you'll start living like a king. It could, however, mean that you'll become the CEO of a company that provides the solution to a problem facing your community. Or you may become a volunteer for an important cause and end up making a significant impact on the lives of others.

A healthy pride

Pride all too often has negative connotations, expressed in the famous quote from the Bible: 'Pride goeth before the fall.' It's often confused with vanity or egotism. Yet we also know that a person with unhealthy low self-esteem seldom lives a happy and fruitful life. Confidence, respect, and acceptance of our authentic self are beneficial traits when it comes to being of service to the world. Only a balanced individual can help bring balance to the world, and healthy pride is an essential part of that.

Deities have pride in spades and fortunately it'll rub off on us when we have a relationship with one of them. A good example are the Orishas of the Yoruba Ifa religions that made the journey from West Africa to the Americas alongside the captured people on the slave ships. The ability of these people to keep their gods and goddesses alive, sometimes by syncretizing them with Catholic saints to hide them from their oppressors, helped them to survive. And nowadays the Orisha are inspiring a new sense of (healthy) pride in African ancestry, history, and culture.

The desire to leave a legacy

The last of the main gifts deities give us is the desire to leave a legacy. In this sense, the legacy isn't the result of vanity or egotism, but of a strong sense of purpose. Even though some other types of spirit guide can be involved and invested in our life purpose, deities take this calling to another level with the desire to build something that lasts. It's true that some people will translate this urge into building huge structures that are visible even from the moon or making some other grand gesture that may or may not be in the best interest of their community. But on a deeper level, the urge to leave a legacy is really about departing the Earth plane knowing that your efforts have made this world a better place for future inhabitants. Entrepreneurs, CEOs, high-level politicians, and famous artists, actors, and musicians are great examples of people with the dedication, discipline, and urge to succeed that will result in leaving a legacy of value.

This doesn't mean that you have to be famous or build a million-dollar company to leave a legacy (unless you want to). For you, the desire to leave a legacy might be expressed in a website dedicated to your personal hobby, e.g. Chinese poetry from the 1600s. Or it could be meticulously researching your family tree for future generations to enjoy. A personal example would be this book, which is my contribution to the study of spirit communication.

Challenges

Since we live in a dualistic world, everything we do can have positive and negative consequences. While we can look forward to enjoying the benefits our spirit guides bring us, we also need to be aware of the challenges they may present so that we can avoid the pitfalls. When it comes to deities, who have human-like personalities and therefore struggle with some of the same challenges we do (only on a bigger scale), there are three main risks we need to look out for and avoid because they can potentially inflate our ego and therefore place us on the wrong path.

Blind devotion

Challenge number one can result in suffering for us and others, especially if we follow false gods or ideals. Earlier in this chapter we talked about how deities demand devotion. While this is true, please know that they would never ask you to follow them blindly into a life of despair.

So how do you know if you're talking to one of the benevolent gods or if you're being manipulated by a being who doesn't have your best interest at heart? I'll go into this in more depth in Part III, but first and foremost, trust your instincts. Listen to your intuition and enter into a relationship with a deity just as you would with a human being – slowly and carefully. Don't promise lifelong dedication to someone you hardly know! Take your time to get to know them and take note of the effect the new relationship has on your life. If you feel an overall improvement and sense of happiness, you can risk taking the next step. If you seem to be caught in a downward spiral of unpleasant events, be cautious and distance yourself from this spirit.

Becoming power-hungry

Working with a deity lets you experience a potentiality much bigger than your own and can leave you wanting more. There's certainly nothing wrong with taking on more responsibility in order to influence and improve the world. But you must do it with the right intentions and keep your ego in check. Otherwise, this striving can turn into an ugly case of self-importance. You might find yourself putting your own needs above those of others because, after, all, *you* were chosen by the gods and therefore have the right to make decisions on their behalf without considering their wants and needs. This pattern has led to disastrous results throughout history – it can and has ended in wars, colonialism, persecution, and genocide. So how can we avoid this pitfall?

The easiest way is to watch other people's reactions to your ideas and actions. If they put their trust in you and happily follow your lead, you have nothing to fear. However, if they regularly cut you out of the decision-making process because they don't believe that you have everyone's best interest at heart, it's time to pause, reflect, and make the needed adjustments to your behavior. Deity guides can and do help you stay clear of this ego trap by guiding you into situations that require you to become more responsible for yourself and others. But you need to remain attuned to your shared purpose and keep your own ego in check in order to fulfill your promise and become an effective and respected leader.

Chasing immortality

The quest for immortality is as old as humanity itself and still influences our daily lives. You only have to look at all the anti-aging products lining the shelves and flooding our feeds online, or the prevalence of plastic surgery, to see what I mean. But where does this desire to live forever come from?

Think about it: most gods and goddesses are immortal (at least from our perspective) and so what happens is some people start wanting that for themselves as well. However, this desire is dangerous, since immortality keeps us from advancing toward our destiny. Death is just a portal of transformation that delivers us to the next stage of our journey. Not wanting to pass through it keeps us stuck in a mode of being that doesn't suit our soul growth. We can overcome this challenge by being open to change in all its forms, consciously dealing with death, and recognizing that we're immortal on a soul level and therefore don't have to be in our physical form.

Gods and goddesses assist us with this challenge by giving us glimpses of the world on the other side of the veil where, one day, we'll all end up. These impressions help us recognize that there's much more to be experienced in these other dimensions after leaving the physical plane behind. So, if you start sensing a growing desire, fueled by self-importance, to defy mortality, it's time to check in with your deity guide and humbly reconnect to your purpose while here on Earth.

What does your connection to a deity say about you?

Now that you've learnt what deities are and become familiar with their unique characteristics, gifts, and challenges, let's take a step back and examine what it says about *you* when one of your spirit guides is a god or goddess. What does your connection to them tell you about yourself?

You have a clear sense of purpose

Before you protest that you don't know what your life purpose *is*, even though you've been looking for it for years, let me reassure you that your soul knows exactly why you're here. It knows that you aren't just in it for your own growth and enjoyment. You decided to come here on a mission to make this world a better place, using the specific skills and talents you've developed over lifetimes. So even if you feel lost and stuck sometimes, your higher self knows exactly what needs to be done. It's just your human self that struggles, because it tends to want all the answers *now*.

All lightworkers who are here now have a sense of purpose, regardless of the identity of their spirit guides, but with a deity guide, your commitment and dedication will allow you to make a bigger impact than most. Through the connection with that guide, you're able to get the bigger-picture view, develop the power needed for the job, and cultivate the leadership abilities to get everyone on board, ultimately leaving a lasting legacy for your community.

You have charisma

Even though contemporary kings and queens have a mostly ceremonial role, back in the day they were the most influential people in the country. When they did a good job, they provided their people with guidance, inspiration, and entertainment. Nowadays, the most influential people are those we see daily in the media: movie stars, athletes, big-shot CEOs, and political leaders. But here's the secret: their rise to the top didn't only happen because of their skills. Often, it was also because of their charisma.

The Merriam-Webster dictionary defines 'charisma' as 'a personal magic of leadership arousing special popular loyalty or enthusiasm for a public figure.' In other words, it's a type of devotion-inducing leadership seen as extraordinary. From a spiritual perspective, it's a quality of soul that allows someone to be a guiding light. It allows them to illuminate the way for a group of people who trust that they'll help them create better lives. Even though you might not know it yet, you have charisma as well. If you still have doubts, replace *charisma* with *presence* and think back to times in your life when people felt drawn to you because of your presence.

Creating a closer connection with your personal god or goddess will bring this out. They chose to work with you because, as mentioned earlier, you have a similar energy signature that draws the two of you together. Part of this is your charisma. Working with them also increases this presence, because you're learning from them how it works and how you can apply it in your own life. And lastly, taking on responsibility as a leader allows you to develop charisma over time.

You have the will to exert power for the benefit of all

Has anyone ever called you bossy, overbearing, or pushy? These characteristics are often seen as negative, but in a different light, they mean that you have the will to exert power to reach your goals. Having a deity as a spirit guide shows that you have at least the potential to utilize your will to exert power for the benefit of all. This is an extraordinary quality that's meant to be used with only the best of intentions. Please know that I'm not talking about forcing anyone to do something they don't want to do. This is about harnessing your personal power to help yourself and others bring more light into the world. You have this potential when a deity guide is at your side.

Deity communication across cultures

When it comes to the cultures and spiritual traditions that have worked with deities throughout history, three of the best known are the ancient Greek, Roman, and Indian civilizations. We've all heard of Mars and Aphrodite, and seen at least one statue of Neptune with his trident at the center of a fountain. And most spiritually minded folks also know about Ganesh, the elephant-headed remover of obstacles who has made the trip from India to altars around the world.

However, gods and goddesses can be found worldwide, from Japan to Nigeria and Brazil to Cambodia. We don't even have to go back in history to learn how people connect and communicate with deities. Contemporary examples can be found in Revival Paganism, African-diasporic religions like Vodou and Candomblé, as well as the spirituality movement sweeping Western culture. Individuals from these spiritual communities have taught and written books on the subject as well. Tanishka and Sophie Bashford come to mind, along with Diana L. Paxson, as well as Kenaz Filan and Raven Kaldera, among many others.

Most spiritual traditions working with deities communicate with them through ritual, ceremony, prayer, and organized group worship. Offerings can be a big part of this, because making an offering creates a sense of reciprocity between you and the deity, and between the spiritual and physical worlds. Offerings differ depending on the spiritual practice, but all show appreciation of the deity involved. You might like to connect with your deity guide by building a small altar in your home and making offerings of small objects that are meaningful to you.

To give you an idea, in the Shinto religion a common offering is a glass of *sake*, which signifies a bountiful and blessed harvest. In Hinduism, offerings of fresh flowers are used to adorn an altar, and in Candomblé, worshippers cook specific foods to offer to their gods and goddesses on special occasions. The spiritual practice of animal sacrifice also comes from the tradition of offerings. While I'm a vegetarian and don't wish to make these kinds of offering, it's important to respect different traditions around the world and not judge based on Western ideals. Traditions practicing animal sacrifice have included the ancient Greeks, Romans, Egyptians, and Aztecs. Mostly, the sacrificed animals weren't wasted, but served as a sacred meal to ritual participants or people in need.

Receiving the call

Spirit workers throughout history and across the world who have a deity as their spirit guide have received the call to work with them in the following ways:

- a fascination with one of the spiritual traditions that worship deities

- an unseen presence that almost demands their attention

- an ancestral connection to a specific god or goddess

- repeated synchronicities that involve the deity

- dreams that feature this type of guide

The deity relationship can take on the nature of that between parent and child, employer and employee, commander and soldier, lover and beloved, or friend and friend. The degree of involvement with a deity spirit guide can range from a loose connection to full-on possession. The latter has nothing to do with evil spirits, but simply means that the human allows the deity to use their body to perform healing, participate in rituals, or give guidance to members of the community. Whatever form your connection takes, remember that both parties benefit from it. You, the human, assist the deity in achieving their objectives on Earth, and in return they give you blessings and gifts to guide your spiritual advancement and bring you fulfilling life experiences.

It's up to you to create a unique communication style to use to converse with your spirit guide. Consider what you've learnt in this chapter. Which parts resonated with you on an intuitive level? Which parts didn't make much sense to you? And what would you like to try or learn more about? If you wish, you can make notes in your workbook (*see Bonuses, p.243*), ready for when you get to create your own ritual to connect with the specific deity you're working with.

DEITIES AT A GLANCE

Characteristics: Authoritative, demanding devotion, involved in human affairs

Gifts: Leadership skills, a healthy pride, the desire to leave a legacy

Challenges: Blind devotion, becoming power-hungry, chasing immortality

What having this type of spirit guide says about you: You have a clear sense of purpose, charisma, and the will to exert power for the benefit of all!

Next, we'll look at ancestors – their characteristics, gifts, challenges, and how humans have worked with them throughout history and across cultures.

~

CHAPTER 5

ƆNCESTORS

I prayed and meditated to ready myself. Then I called Darla, an ancestral healer. I hoped to connect with an ancestor guide who could help me shed light on the mystery of my origins. We'd concentrate on one birth lineage during this session and work with the others, including those of my adoptive ancestors, later. Since I'd always felt close to my indigenous roots, I expected my birth mother's lineage to come through and work with us that day. I was in for a big surprise.

Darla asked me to use my intuition to scan for ancestors willing to aid us. When I did, I felt a wave of love and joy washing over me and I beamed from ear to ear. It felt as if I was receiving a big loving hug. Next, with my inner vision, I saw an elderly lady of African descent sitting in front of a huge cooking pot under a clear sky. She smiled at me and encouraged me to take a seat across from her. I'd never seen her before, but based on her ethnicity, I realized that my birth father's mother's lineage had connected with me.

Now you need to realize that I had no information about my birth father, let alone his ancestors. I still don't know his name, his age, what he does or did for a living, or even if he's still alive. The only thing I came to suspect over time was that he was of African ancestry, one of the many descendants of enslaved West Africans in Colombia. I came to this conclusion after repeated family visits to the USA as a teenager, starting when I was 12 years old. There, as I related earlier, I felt instantly at home and African-Americans treated me like one of their own. It was as if I belonged to a secret club the rest of my family weren't a part of. This baffled me because I'd never considered myself black, and nor had anyone else.

But the lady who stepped forward to be my ancestral guide on my father's mother's side was of African descent. Connecting with her made me realize that the African-Americans had been correct about my heritage and it settled something inside me. I remembered the people who had thought my lips weren't full enough and my nose not broad enough to be of African origin. They had never realized how hurtful (and ignorant) their comments were. And I'd kept quiet because I couldn't prove it. But now I knew and didn't care what anyone else said. Tears of joy started streaming down my face because I realized that there was a reason why I was drawn to African spirituality and that I alone got to define who I was, no matter what other people thought. I remain grateful for this lesson from my ancestor guide.

A few weeks before, I'd taken a DNA test, and 14 days after this session with Darla I got the results via email. I opened my inbox with unsteady hands. What if I was mistaken after all? I took a deep breath and started reading. With a sigh of relief, I saw that I was 30 percent of African parentage. I smiled and sent a telepathic message to my new ancestral guide, thanking her and letting her know that I'd always honor her legacy, no matter what.

What exactly are ancestors?

Ancestors are those who have lived before us and are no longer with us on the physical plane. This includes our grandparents and great-grandparents and other family members we've known in this lifetime. However, it further includes family members who lived hundreds or thousands of years ago and have been forgotten by history, as well as ancestors from previous lifetimes.

In a larger sense, our ancestors comprise those who made us the person we are today. Not just via transferring DNA to us, but also on vocational, cultural, intellectual, emotional, and spiritual levels. Our ancestors include the authors of books that have inspired us, the founders of our culture or religion, and the individuals who made substantial advancements in our profession. In an even wider definition, all the humans who lived before us are our ancestors, no matter when or where they lived or what their beliefs were.

Which leaves us with a conundrum to solve. Can every single ancestor become a spirit guide? What about the rapists, murderers, addicts, compulsive liars, and narcissists? We all have them among our ancestors if we go back far enough. Don't worry, most societies and sacred traditions around the world acknowledge these more unpleasant spirits and have ways to cope with them. They don't take their guidance or advice, because they're not spirit guide material! However, we often inherit the unresolved issues that these ancestors grappled with during their life. Alcoholism, abuse, and poverty are examples of this. I know, this sounds unfair. Why should we have to clean up other people's mess? The reason is that our souls agreed to help heal these issues before we incarnated. We made a commitment to our lineage, including ourselves, the troubled souls, the coming generations, and our ancestor guides. We agreed to clean up the mess so that everyone can enjoy the gifts and blessings that can then be passed down the lineage, unhindered by karmic obstacles.

Even though several ancestors may have left us with problems, ancestors who have matured enough can become our guides and will be helping us fix them. Remember my interpretation of spirit guides? It only includes those from the higher spheres who connect to us in unconditional love and want to encourage us on our spiritual path.

How do you know if an ancestor is acting as a cosmic helper? By taking your time in establishing a relationship with them, just as you would with a deity and with someone here in the physical world. You don't welcome just anyone into your house and do whatever they say, right? You take things slowly and observe their behavior. If they treat you with kindness and give you valuable advice over an extended period, it's a go. If they're aggressive and abusive, you avoid them! It's crucial not to follow a dead relative's guidance just because they're a dead relative. It's important to realize that some ancestor spirits have highly developed knowledge and some don't. Only those that do can become our guides.

This is true even if our ancestors were delightful people on the Earth plane. They'll still be delightful and may also have gained some new insights and had the chance to grow and evolve since their passing. But death doesn't necessarily transform anyone into a wise, loving, and all-knowing being. So, Uncle Harry, who never read a book in his life, can't help you write your dissertation. But if he had a knack for getting along with children, he's the right person to ask for support if your son's having a hard time making friends at school.

Guide characteristics

Besides having a higher perspective on life than living humans, ancestor guides also share three other qualities. Let's look at these now.

A strong sense of family bonds

Ancestor guides know that families are the human equivalent of soul pods. Soul pods are groups of souls who travel through time and space together like a pack of wolves or a herd of elephants. They have a shared purpose, such as bringing more laughter into the world or serving as guardians. So they may incarnate as a family of entertainers, for example, or one that provides their community with generations of law-enforcement personnel. Soul pod members enjoy a tight bond. Some of your pod members might be your actual family members. Others might be in your inner circle because of a powerful heart-to-heart connection and a sense of instant familiarity. They're your soulmates (which is different from romantic twin-flame relationships).

Remember this famous line from the movie *Lilo and Stitch*? '*Ohana* means family. Family means nobody gets left behind or forgotten.' That's how your soul family feels about you. Soul families can include not only our family members of blood but also the people who are like family on a soul level.

Ancestor guides recognize how important it is to keep all family members healthy, happy, and connected, so they can help one another grow, evolve, and live their purpose.

A desire to maintain the bloodline or spiritual lineage

Imagine you're part of a team that's working on a critical mission, like bringing peace to a region, healing an incurable illness, or introducing new technology. You realize it'll take generations to reach your goal, so you find and train like-minded people to continue your work. You have a strong desire to guide these successors, and provide them with tips, tools, and resources to help them along the way. You want to maintain the lineage. The same is true for your ancestor guides. They're always around trying to help bring out the skills, talents, and gifts available in both your soul and family lineages.

Sometimes these inherited blessings are obvious to spot. If your grandmother and your mother were drawn to work with children and you are as well, it's clear that your soul pod's bigger purpose is to shape the minds and hearts of future generations. However, sometimes it's harder to identify the common thread. An example from my own life is that my father (technically my adoptive father but to me he's just my father) worked in space technology and I've studied astrology for 15 years. These are two different approaches, but they both explore the same subject.

Enormous wisdom

Imagine all the accumulated life experiences of all your ancestors. They've seen it all and done it all – the good, the bad, and everything in between. Each new generation can access this knowledge via their subconscious and their DNA. But because of the modern-day disconnection from our lineages on a spiritual level, we don't mobilize this information to use it for our own improvement.

Real ancestral guides earned their status by turning this tremendous knowledge pool into wisdom. They committed to continuous growth as a soul and to transforming their own human experiences and karma into wisdom for the soul pod, humanity at large, and all living beings. Through them, you can enjoy it as well and gain tremendous intuitive insights that you can use in your own personal life, including finding and living your purpose.

Gifts

Your ancestor guides bring gifts they wish to share with you. These are varied and unique for each lineage. They can include physical abilities, like being able to run fast, intellectual capacities such as comprehending large amounts of information, and emotional talents like empathy. Let's examine some common gifts that all ancestor guides bring.

Access to the wisdom of our lineage

Earlier we touched upon the fact that our ancestor guides have an enormous amount of wisdom we can draw upon to improve our life. This gift isn't just meant for our own betterment but to share with others so they can enjoy it too. Through this act of giving and experiencing life through the eyes of the people we're helping, we add to our soul pod's wealth of knowledge.

An example from my life would be that I enjoy sharing the wisdom of my indigenous ancestors, who perceived all life as sentient, be it a human being, an animal, a plant, a rock, or even the weather. This leads to fascinating discussions with people from all walks of life who allow me to experience how they view the world in return. I learn something new every time. When we share our ancestral gifts, it allows us to integrate new lessons and insights into our ancestral wisdom pool.

Family healing

There are no perfect families and some of us have dysfunctional, addicted, abusive, or absent family members. These issues don't affect just one individual pod member. In fact, they're almost always multi-generational. Even so, family healing might not sound like much of a gift. If our parents, siblings, or best friends display unhealthy behavior, it's not our fault, so why do we need to be given healing? The reason is that we share an energy pool with our soulmates, so we suffer from feelings of guilt, shame, and anger as a result. We carry the same seeds in our soul as they do, the good and the bad.

To fix the core problem, we must turn to our ancestral guides. They can point us to when and where in the past the trouble started and how to resolve it. And even though we can't work out others' problems for them, with our guides' help we can resolve the underlying seed issue inside ourselves. The healed energy then flows to our soul pod members in all timelines, past, present, and future. It helps heal everyone involved.

Strong spiritual roots

A gift from our ancestor guides that's much needed in Western society is the rediscovery of our spiritual roots. Many of us turn to other cultures to satisfy our deep hunger for spiritual knowledge, even to the point of making the same mistakes European colonizers made by taking whatever we want without giving back, which can have disastrous consequences for the affected cultures. We don't even stop to wonder where this yearning is coming from. If we examined it further, we'd recognize that our society has cut itself off from its spiritual roots.

Christianity taught us valuable lessons, but it also destroyed the partnership with our Earth-honoring ancestors by condemning and prosecuting anyone who followed the old ways. This resulted in a tremendous loss of knowledge, which we're now seeking abroad. A resumed connection with our ancestor guides can put an end to this and bring healing by restoring the relationship with our original spiritual lineage. This heals the connection to Mother Earth and all her inhabitants and fulfills the desire for an authentic form of spirituality.

Challenges

Besides the gifts we receive from our ancestor guides, there are also challenges to face and overcome. These don't come from our ancestor guides themselves, but from the lineage we share with them, including the ancestors who still have some healing to do. Our job is to tackle these problems and clear the way to growth and expanded wisdom for all members of our soul pod.

Succumbing to the myth of being 'chosen'

Ancient stories of being the 'chosen ones,' the 'real people,' or the 'rightful rulers' foster the assumption that our soul ancestry is better than those of others. Most cultures, traditions, and nations recognize a variant of those stories and have used it as an excuse to discriminate against, violate, and enslave others. This challenge shows up when we try to convince, manipulate, or force someone to live by our family's or community's values and beliefs. This can happen even in small ways like judging others on account of their table manners, their accent, or their skin color.

To avoid this pitfall and deal with the challenge, our ancestral guides encourage us to reach out to people outside our usual circle. Next time you get the chance to attend an event organized by a group of individuals you may have judged in the past, accept the opportunity to explore. See what you can learn from them. You don't have to become best friends, but see if you can find at least one positive takeaway from your experience.

Being overly focused on the past

Another challenge when working with ancestor guides can come up if we focus on the past to the point where we forget that the present and future also need our attention. The good old times during which our ancestors were more connected to the Divine, the world around us, and one another can become an ideal world that we long to recreate. We overlook that this glorified version of bygone times doesn't include the struggles and difficult conditions the ancient ones had to endure.

Our ancestral guides will help us circumvent this challenge by refocusing us on our life purpose and the objectives of our soul pod. Remembering why we incarnated for this lifetime and taking action on it'll ground us in the present. Since our ancestor guides' goal is to continue the lineage, they'll also remind us how paramount it is to work toward a better future for the next generations. This also steers us away from the past.

Traditionalism

Traditionalism also glorifies bygone days and can contribute to current difficulties. There's nothing wrong with valuing traditions that honor the past, support the present, and help shape the future. However, traditionalism can become a fear-based mechanism to resist necessary change and development. You could wash all your clothes by hand in the river because that's how your ancestors did their laundry, and that could be a fun experiment to try, but it would keep you from other priorities. Time playing with your children, keeping up with your job, and practicing basic self-care could all suffer.

Our ancestral guides don't expect us to recreate the traditions and daily rituals they established during their time on Earth. Instead, they call on us to focus on the core lessons they learnt and tailor them to our own lifestyle.

What does your connection to an ancestor guide say about you?

After familiarizing yourself with ancestor guides, it's now time to turn the spotlight on yourself. What does it say about *you* when one of your top three spirit guides is an ancestor, according to the quiz? What does your connection tell you about yourself? People who work with ancestor guides a lot share three attributes.

You're a family person

A close relationship with an ancestor guide can show that you value family. Yes, you might be dealing with a difficult situation at home and finding family members taking up your time, standing in your way, or trying to keep you down. However, these problems show that you are indeed a family person. Why else would you worry so much while other family members are much less anxious about the situation? It might be your soul calling you to help clear up these issues so that your whole family and soul pod can enjoy your relationships with each other.

Basically, you value family and all it represents. You want to be part of a happy, healthy, and thriving family unit. If that's not the reality you're living in now, that doesn't mean that keeping the family together, healing family karma, and passing on family wisdom isn't part of your life purpose. In fact, it shows that it is. Someone who cares about these matters is the perfect soul to heal a problematic family situation.

You're passionate about history and record-keeping

Working closely with an ancestor spirit means you have a keen interest in the past. It could be super-specific, like an obsession with family genealogy, past lives, Egyptology, or the history of knitting. It could also manifest as a general respect for anything old and historic. Either way, you're passionate about history and record-keeping because deep down in your heart you know that studying the past helps you create a better future.

Your ancestor guide will equip you with a direct connection to the wisdom of those who walked this path before you. However, understand that it's you who is in charge now. Your guide is there to advise you, but you're the one who has incarnated at this point in history. It's up to you to make final decisions about where you want to go in life and lead the way.

You enjoy a powerful connection to the land

Like people who are connected to nature spirits, if you have an ancestor as a main guide, you have a great relationship with Mother Earth. Nature spirits teach us we're all part of a community of beings that share the same planet. Ancestor guides remind us we're all literally walking on our predecessors' bones and that they were the ones who helped shape this planet. So, you'll find the Earth grounds you and makes you feel connected and safe.

Your love for Mother Earth can encompass the entire planet or focus on a distinct place, but the closer you become to your ancestor guide, the stronger your respect for the Earth will be. You'll take on the role of caretaker and protector of the land and won't want to see it destroyed or exploited for the short-term benefit of a few. You might even sense ley lines, energy vortexes, the locations of valuable resources, and similar places of power. Just follow your intuition or use a dowsing rod and see where it leads.

Ancestor communication across cultures

Almost all cultures have developed a way to bond with their ancestors. Only a few assume that our last breath is the absolute end. The rest believe in an afterlife in another place, be it the heaven or hell in Catholicism, the Valhalla of Norse mythology, or the watery world beneath our own of the Emberá in Colombia. Buddhism, Sikhism, Spiritism (not to be confused with Spiritualism!), Theosophy and many other spiritual traditions also subscribe to reincarnation.

Funeral rites and ceremonies help us bid farewell to those who have died. They also exist to facilitate their journey to the land of the ancestors, as seen in ancient Egypt. In addition, they make certain that those passing into the spirit world remember the good deeds of those of us still on Earth. In return, we hope to enlist their help when needed. This can be seen in many sub-Saharan African societies.

We can contact ancestor spirits on our own or with the help of a professional who has become a specialist by either vocation or training. If you live in the Western world, you might know these experts as mediums, but please recognize that each culture and spiritual tradition has its own terminology and customs. In some parts of Japan they call such people *itako*, among the Shona in Zimbabwe they're known *masvikiro*, and the Maori in New Zealand refer to them as *matakite*.

The techniques used to connect with ancestor guides also vary. Prayer, fasting, offerings, dance, meditation, divination tools, and entheogenic plants are all popular, but the goal is the same: to reach a trance state. It can range from light to deep and last from a few minutes to several hours. During this altered state, spirit workers either wait for an ancestor spirit to speak up or they travel to the afterworld to find the spirit to whom they wish to speak.

Even in contemporary, Westernized, metropolitan population centers all over the world, people consult professional mediums daily, often through Spiritualism, a Christian religion based on the assumption that humans can communicate with the deceased. Their Sunday services include demonstrations where a medium relays messages from passed loved ones to members of the congregation. Spiritualist churches also provide classes for anybody who wishes to learn mediumship skills.

In Stansted, in the UK, for example, the Spiritualists' National Union runs mediumship workshops at the world-renowned Arthur Findlay College. Here you can learn to communicate with your own loved ones or develop into a professional medium who does readings for others. My favorite center for mediumship training, however, is the Sir Arthur Conan Doyle Centre in Edinburgh, where I continue to enhance my skills in mediumship. There are also independent mediumship teachers like Gordon Smith, Tony Stockwell, and James Van Praagh. They were all trained in the Spiritualist tradition but have since formed their own approach.

There are many other ancestral specialists available. Dr. Daniel Foor, a teacher and practitioner of practical animism, specializes in ancestral and family healing. He's explored several spiritual traditions, including Neo-Paganism, Mongolian Shamanism,

Islamic Sufism, Mahayana Buddhism, and West African Ifá. His ancestral healing system focuses on identifying and connecting with what he calls 'the well ancestors.' They're the forebears who have evolved enough to turn into ancestor guides.

We also have Malidoma Somé, an author and teacher born into a Dagara community from Burkina Faso, who has shared the wisdom of his ancestors for 20 years. He brings a message of hope, healing, and reconciliation through the powerful tools of ritual and community-building.

It's up to you to create a unique communication style to use to converse with your spirit guide. Consider what you learnt in this chapter. Which parts resonated with you on an intuitive level? Which parts didn't make much sense to you? And what would you like to try or learn more about? If you wish, you can make notes in your workbook (*see Bonuses, p.243*), ready for when you get to create your own ritual to connect with the specific ancestor you're working with.

Receiving the call

Spirit workers throughout history and across the world who have had an ancestor as one of their spirit guides have received the call to work with them in the following ways:

- a fascination with one of the spiritual traditions that worship ancestors

- an unseen presence that feels like someone familiar

- an ancestral connection to ancestor veneration

- repeated synchronicities that involve an ancestor

- dreams that feature this type of spirit guide

ANCESTORS AT A GLANCE

Characteristics: A strong sense of family bonds, a desire to continue the bloodline or spiritual lineage, enormous wisdom

Gifts: Access to the wisdom of our lineage, family healing, strong spiritual roots

Challenges: Succumbing to the myth of being 'chosen', being too focused on the past, traditionalism

What having this type of spirit guide says about you: You're a family person, you're passionate about history and record-keeping, you enjoy a powerful connection to the land.

Next, we'll look at ascended masters – their characteristics, gifts, challenges, what having one as a spirit guide says about you, and how humans have worked with them throughout history and across cultures.

∼

CHAPTER 6

ASCENDED MASTERS

Trance mediumship can take many forms. The best known is trance speaking, which is when a medium lets a spirit guide take control of their voice to speak through them. You can liken the experience to being relegated to the back seat of your own car while someone else is driving. You know what's happening, but have no influence over it. I've only experienced this twice. The second time, I connected with a soul residing in the realm of the ascended masters.

After doing my usual spirit guide meditation, I listened to a guided meditation created by the famous British medium Tony Stockwell. His voice took me deeper and deeper into myself. It reminded me of when I'd undergone surgery, when slipping away after receiving the anesthesia had felt like diving into a deep black sea of nothingness. Only this time, I stayed conscious while sinking into a velvety, calming space.

After a while, the recording directed me to sweep the energetic space around me to see if a spirit was willing to communicate through me. As this was my first attempt at trance mediumship, I didn't expect to get any results, but to my utter surprise I received an image in my mind's eye right away: a teenage girl, maybe 14 years old, sitting in the lotus position. Her head was shaven, she was wearing a dark red Buddhist robe and she had a huge smile on her face.

Telepathically, she told me that she'd lived in Nepal. She'd had psychic abilities and her parents hadn't known what to do with her and had even been a little afraid of her, so they had taken her to a Buddhist temple that took on such children. She'd spent most of her life there before passing away at a young age. She'd been on a mission with her teacher, an older monk who had taken her along to help and learn, and they had been crossing a mountain when a rockfall ended their lives. She relayed all this background information about herself as a quick introduction. I then felt compelled to open my mouth and let her speak through me.

I listened to my own voice explaining she was part of a group of souls who had all died young and therefore kept the knowledge of what it was like to be a young human. Now, led by a group of ascended masters, they were preparing to serve the next generation of humans born with heightened spiritual abilities. These children would need skilled spirit guides who could help them fulfill their missions. She spoke of the importance of letting our young ones know that it's normal and okay to have psychic, shamanic, and mediumistic experiences. They also need to learn to use these skills to serve others.

Since I wasn't a teenager anymore, I wondered why she'd come to me and how I could help. She laughed and told me that her group of future spirit guides was currently practicing contacting incarnated human spirit workers. This would help them later when it was time to communicate with the kids they would serve. I'd simply been available and tuned in when she'd started her practice session. In fact it was the first attempt at trance mediumship for both of us. She seemed pleased that it had worked out so well. We smiled at each other and then burst out giggling like teenage girls do. When Tony's voice called me back into my body, we said goodbye with a mental high five and a big smile.

What exactly are ascended masters?

Ascended masters are human beings who have gained the wisdom and mastery needed to reach enlightenment and have ascended. This means they've merged with their higher selves, are free from karma and need not incarnate anymore. Instead, they reside in the sixth dimension or above and assist us from there.

The term 'ascended master' was first coined by Baird T. Spalding in 1924 in his series of books *The Life and Teachings of the Masters of the Far East*. However, I believe these evolved souls have existed since the beginning of human history and in every culture people have known them by one name or another.

During their lifetimes, these souls became masters of their own spiritual traditions or took an individual path and paved the way for others to follow. There are more famous ascended masters and a countless number of lesser-known or even unknown ones. Gautama Buddha is a great example of a well-known master, and millions still follow his teachings. Jesus and Mohammed, the respective founders of Christianity and Islam, are also ascended masters who have a huge influence on lives all around the world today. One example of a female ascended master is Mary Magdalene. No, she wasn't a prostitute, and the Church officially recognized this in 1969. Others are the beloved Buddhist bodhisattva Guan Yin, and Lady Nada, who lived in Atlantis and is the unifier of families and twin flames.

Many ascended masters are long forgotten by history, but countless saints, priests, gurus, nuns, and other spiritual teachers have taken the path to enlightenment and still serve humanity from behind the veil. Many will forever remain unnamed because they held no important positions and had no social status. Some spent their entire lives meditating in a cave and others simply dedicated their lives to the relief of human suffering wherever and however they could. What they all share now is that they won't return to Earth for another incarnation. They've moved on beyond the fifth dimension and therefore make great spirit guides and wayshowers for us.

An important fact to remember about ascended masters is that each one works with many individuals simultaneously, so no one can claim to be the only person guided by one particular master. Their main concern is humanity at large and how to help us raise our vibration to the point of enlightenment. Each one of them is responsible for a certain task that needs to be accomplished, like bringing peace, releasing karma, cultivating compassion, etc.

They lead groups of people who all share that mission and have complementary personalities. You can think of a group like this as a spiritual task force or crew. So, if you meet someone who has the same ascended master as a spirit guide, there should be no competition between you. Take it as a sign that you're on the right path, because you've met someone from your soul crew. Share your experiences and compare notes!

Guide characteristics

Even though each ascended master is an individual and therefore has their own personality traits and teaches their own particular lessons, there are certain characteristics that set ascended masters apart as a group. Understanding these will help you identify and connect with your personal ascended master guide later on.

A wealth of knowledge about life on Earth

You can recognize an ascended master by the dignified energy that surrounds them. Encountering one exposes you to the enormous wisdom they've gained through their countless lives lived on Mother Earth and other planets. Along with ancestor spirits, this type of spirit guide is closest to us in the sense that they know what it's like to live life as an incarnated soul. They have a wealth of knowledge about life on Earth because they've experienced the highs and the lows, and the variety. Ascended masters have incarnated as men, women, transgender and non-binary people, and anything in between. They've lived in many countries, cultures, and epochs. They've studied multiple spiritual traditions and have learnt that, at the core, they're all based on the same spiritual principles. They've walked many paths and attained a wealth of knowledge and experience that over time has turned into wisdom. They've discovered how to merge the ego with the higher self, which is what ascension and enlightenment are all about, and this characteristic makes them great spirit guides. The difference between ascended master and ancestor guides is that ascended masters are highly evolved souls, whereas some ancestors still have much to learn and can assist us only to a certain point.

Compassion for the human journey

This type of spirit guide is closest to us in the sense that they realize how rough it can be for us. Ascended masters have been able to release all their karma and leave the reincarnation cycle. But during their lives on Earth, they've made every mistake possible. They know what it's like to live in fear and to experience jealousy, greed, selfishness, rage, and deep despair. They've been cruel to others and to themselves. Because of that, they can relate to the struggles we go through on our way to enlightenment and have immense compassion for the human journey. They'll never judge us or make us feel bad about the decisions we've made. Instead, they encourage us to recognize that we all make mistakes and that forgiveness for ourselves and others is the way forward. Even if it takes several lifetimes to release all our karma and find our own path through the different dimensions to ascension and enlightenment.

Ascended masters know how hard this can be, but they also know what makes the incarnation journey easier and more joyful and are happy to pass it on to make our path a little easier. The chance to work with an ascended master is therefore very rewarding in the sense that it can save us from making the same mistakes they made. If we'll listen!

The ability to connect people with their higher self

Enlightenment is the merging of our human self (our ego) with our higher self. All ascended masters have reached this state, so they're very competent in guiding us toward this goal. They teach us that the trick isn't to fight the ego but to recognize that it's a necessary part of our physical existence. It tries to keep us safe by avoiding change, but it'll do so at all costs, even if that means using counterintuitive measures like leading us into addiction, hanging on to trauma, or falling into depression. Yes, unchecked, the ego can create real havoc in our lives.

An ascended master will help us work with the ego. It can then recognize that its job isn't to keep us safe at all costs but to merge with and assist the higher self. Only if these work together in harmony can we live fulfilled lives, release karma, and move one step at a time toward ascension.

Gifts

There are plenty of gifts that come from working with ascended masters. There are many stories of saints, prophets, and other holy people who had the ability to heal instantly, live without solid food, levitate, or perform other miracles. Each ascended master has different gifts to offer. But let's focus on the three most useful gifts, the ones that can have the most lasting and positive effect on our lives.

Discernment

The first gift I'd like to share with you is the ability to use intuition to discern what deserves your attention and what doesn't. An ascended master has learnt, through multiple incarnations, to let go of any distractions that only serve the ego and create more negative karma. So they can cut through the illusions we can get caught up in. Examples are a negative perception of self, a tendency toward perfectionism, or the fear that we're unlovable.

We have the same ability to discern what's really important and what isn't. Doesn't your intuition tell you where to focus your energy and what not to engage in? You might not always listen, but that little voice tries to guide you daily. This gift becomes stronger the closer your bond to your ascended master guide becomes. It creates a connection between you and your guide that enables you to speed up your spiritual growth beyond anything you can accomplish on your own.

Wisdom

Wisdom is knowledge gained through experience and produces the qualities of unbiased judgment, compassion, self-knowledge, and non-attachment. Ascended masters possess all the above, along with ethics and benevolence, and an ascended master guide can help us find wisdom in our own heart too.

Sometimes wisdom develops when we're going through a difficult life situation that exposes us to the negative expressions of the aforementioned qualities. You may have already experienced intolerance, ignorance, or addiction in your own life or in the lives of those you love and cherish. These excruciating situations are painful, but can be fruitful when you know how to turn them into wisdom. Looking back over your life and recalling the challenges you've faced so far, can you identify the kernel of wisdom you've gained from each one? Put all these in your spiritual toolbox and refer to them often. This is one way you can align yourself with your ascended master guide and create a close relationship with them.

Gratitude

Ascended masters are truly the wisest of those who have gone through the human experience. They perceive the beauty in everything they encounter on their journey and appreciate it as a means of raising their vibration, for they know that gratitude is essential on the path to ascension. An even higher expression of gratitude is to give thanks for the less pleasant experiences of life and the lessons they bring. Remember this, because your ascended master guide has chosen to work with you because they realize that your soul wishes to use gratitude as the path to enlightenment.

Once you practice viewing the world through the eyes of gratitude, you'll notice that you become happier and lighter and things start falling into place. It also becomes easier and easier to connect with your ascended master guide because you're now operating on the same vibrational level. More than that, this gift allows you to make steady progress toward releasing the karma that's holding you back from living your best life.

Challenges

Since we live in a dualistic world, everything we do can have positive and negative consequences. While we can enjoy the benefits our spirit guides bring us, we also need to know the challenges and pitfalls to avoid. With ascended masters, there are three main challenges we need to sidestep because they might lead us down the wrong path.

Living life as an old soul

The fact that one of your spirit guides is an ascended master means that you're an old soul yourself. You've been around the block a few times, which is why you've developed the wonderful gifts we talked about earlier. However, this also comes with its own challenges. You see younger souls following their baser instincts and getting into all kinds of trouble, and you want to let them make their own mistakes without interfering, but this can be hard to do, especially if it's a partner, family member, or friend who is ignoring your sage advice.

To assist you with this, your ascended master guide will lead you into situations where you can teach younger souls. They want you to share your experiences with them rather than telling them what to do. If you're lucky, you yourself have a wise elder in your life you can use as a role model. If not, study the lives of those you admire who lived before you. Notice how these people taught by example and let their actions speak for them instead of instructing others what to do.

Ungratefulness and betrayal from others

Another challenge you face as an old soul is being disappointed by people you trust. This happens because you forget that younger souls often still fall for the many trappings of the ego. Your ascended master guide can help you learn not to take this personally. Instead, reflect on your own journey, recognize where you treated others unkindly, and practice patience and forgiveness. Your guide's vast experience as an incarnated human being will have taught them that the negative behavior of other people says more about these people than about them. Learn from this and be ready to forgive others for their ungratefulness and betrayal.

The solution is to tune in to others intuitively and assess what kind of soul you're dealing with. You wouldn't be as mad at a five-year-old who ate the last piece of chocolate as you would at a 55-year-old, would you? Extend the same courtesy to younger souls. Ascended masters are great at seeing a soul for who they are instead of falling for the illusions their ego might be projecting. They've learnt to see beyond the biggest illusion of all: the notion we're separate from one another and the Universe. So they can show you how to pierce the illusion of ungratefulness and betrayal.

Feeling 'tired of life'

The third challenge that comes from working with an ascended master as a spirit guide is being 'tired of life.' Do you ever sense that you have the weight of the world on your shoulders? Or do you suffer from depression? These can be indications you're facing this challenge. As an old soul, you've seen it all before. That can be tiring. And yes, carrying certain responsibilities *is* part of your life as an old soul, but that doesn't mean that you need to experience it as suffering and misery. Your ascended master guide will help you shake your life up from time to time and have fun.

They'll also guide you into situations where life forces you to let go of burdens that aren't yours to carry. They'll inspire you to let others own their own responsibilities. Your job is to lighten up. The solution to this challenge lies in sharing your life's lessons with others so they can learn and you can share some responsibilities.

What does your connection to an ascended master say about you?

You've learnt what an ascended master is and are familiar with their unique characteristics, gifts, and challenges. Let's examine what it says about *you* when one of your spirit guides is an ascended master. What does your connection tell you about yourself?

You're a great teacher

Since you work with an ascended master as a spirit guide and are an old soul yourself, you make a great teacher. Your wisdom allows others to learn from the life lessons you can share with them. Teaching can take many forms. You could train conscious companies in the newest marketing strategies or write books about how to knit yellow sweaters with green polka dots. Either way, you have knowledge that can enhance the lives of others.

Nowadays, there are various ways of teaching that weren't available to previous generations. Modern technology allows us to connect and work with people across the globe. So, use your creativity in fulfilling this part of your purpose. The simple act of sharing the solutions to your own trials and tribulations on social media can make someone else's day a little easier. Your ascended master guide is ready to assist you in this and to send you the signs, symbols, and synchronicities that will set you on the right path.

You have lots of knowledge from past lives

An archeologist digs up the past to uncover lost knowledge. You can dig up lost knowledge you gathered in past lives and stored in the depths of your soul. This isn't always as available to you as your conscious memories of places you've been and people you've seen, but your higher self forgets nothing. And neither does your ascended master guide, especially as these guides work with people over several lifetimes.

This knowledge often shows up as an intuitive feeling or insight that pops into your head just at the right time to solve a problem you're facing. Sometimes it hides behind an irrational fear that you have to release on your way to ascension. It's not about being able to recall exact details of your previous lifetimes, it's more about recognizing that you have an unconscious reservoir of knowledge and wisdom to fall back on when necessary. Working with an ascended master means that you only need awareness of this to take advantage of it.

You possess a strong sense of responsibility

Younger souls might try to avoid responsibility, but not you! You sometimes see others navigating life with seeming ease and wish you could do the same. But as an elder soul, you have a duty to guide the younger ones. How do I know this? Your ascended master chose to work with you because of your sense of responsibility. They left the reincarnation circle to take on obligations for all humans. All ascended masters now serve as cosmic leaders for others. Your guide chose to be with you to make sure you have all the support you need to fulfill your duties.

What your connection to your ascended master guide says about you is that you're ready to move beyond just caring about yourself and your own dreams and aspirations. You're ready to work for a bigger purpose, which includes the highest good of all humans and all living beings.

Ascended master communication across cultures

At the beginning of this chapter, we defined ascended masters as souls who have lived as humans on Earth, reached enlightenment, and therefore left the reincarnation cycle. This definition includes well-known ascended masters such as Jesus and Buddha. It also includes the many ancestors that reached enlightenment. Keep in mind that they may have lived in cultures and spiritual traditions that use a different term for these elevated souls. Let's now look at how communication with ascended masters works for different people around the globe.

Nowadays, the Catholic Church doesn't acknowledge reincarnation anymore, but it states that certain individuals with a 'sinless soul' (read: without negative karma) can ascend to heaven. Sometimes this even happens in bodily form and is a different process than the usual transition from the embodied state to the heavenly realm. One prominent example is Mary, the mother of Jesus. Her assumption, as the Catholic Church calls her ascension, happened on 15 August and marked the end of her Earthly life. It's not clear if she died first, resurrected after three days, and then ascended into heaven, or if she went straight up without being subjected to the dying process. What we do know is that on the anniversary of her ascension, festivals and parades are held worldwide to celebrate her life in a community setting, while on a more individual level, people light candles and pray to her.

The Yoruba people and some of their neighbors in Nigeria work with the Orishas, which Western anthropologists often identify as gods. However, it's also possible to define at least some of them as ascended masters, since they were once human beings and ascended because of their extraordinary feats. Now they guide humanity (and all of creation) on how to live and succeed on Earth. Communication with the Orishas happens on two levels. One is community based and comprises festivals, ceremonies, and rituals.

Dancing and drumming are used to induce a medium to go into a trance state, which then allows the Orishas to enter their body and express themselves through it. The second level of communication happens at home and includes altars, prayers, and offerings.

In the modern spiritual community, there are many individuals who recognize a connection with one or several ascended masters and use currently popular ways to connect with them. These include oracle cards based on the ascended masters and channeling techniques that allow the spiritual seeker to let their guide speak through them. You can find many of these channeled messages on social media. However, please note that the quality of these channelings differs. To become a reliable channeler, you need training and lots of practice, not just a two-day weekend workshop.

Receiving the call

Spirit workers throughout history and across the world who have had an ascended master as one of their spirit guides have received the call to work with them in the following ways:

- a fascination with one of the spiritual traditions that worship ascended masters

- an unseen presence that comes across as old and wise but human

- an ancestral connection to a specific ascended master

- repeated synchronicities that involve an ascended master

- dreams that feature this type of spirit guide

It's up to you to create a unique communication style to converse with your ascended master spirit guide. Consider what you learnt in this chapter. Which parts resonated with you on an intuitive level? Which parts didn't make much sense to you? And what would you like to try or learn more about? If you wish, you can make notes in your workbook (*see Bonuses, p.243*), ready for when you get to create your own ritual to connect with the specific ascended master you're working with.

ASCENDED MASTERS AT A GLANCE

Characteristics: A wealth of knowledge about life on Earth, compassion for the human journey, the ability to connect people with their higher self

Gifts: Discernment, wisdom, gratitude

Challenges: Living life as an old soul, experiencing ungratefulness and betrayal from others, feeling 'tired of life'

What having this type of spirit guide says about you: You're a great teacher, you have lots of knowledge from past lives, and you have a strong sense of responsibility.

Next, we'll look at nature spirits – their characteristics, gifts, and challenges, what having one as a spirit guide says about you, and how humans have worked with them throughout history and across cultures.

∼

Chapter 7

Nature Spirits

Each evening in Barcelona, people gather to watch the sunset on top of the Turó de la Rovira mountain. The reason is its 360° view of the city, the sea, and the surrounding mountains. It was a strategic site for the defense of the city during the Civil War and later it turned into a shantytown, which it remained until 1990. Now it houses a small museum and has become a popular spot for tourists and locals who want to enjoy the sunset.

I made the trek at least once a week to stay fit, escape the humdrum of the city, and spend some time surrounded by the trees that cover the mountain. One evening, it was busy when I arrived, and people were chatting while munching on the food they had brought and enjoying a cold beer with family and friends, but I found a spot and settled down. Instead of facing the city, I chose to enjoy the view of Montserrat, a holy mountain well known since at least medieval times. The famous monastery on top of it, dedicated to the Holy Virgin, houses a famous Black Madonna.

Right in front of me, the hill sloped down, covered in various plants, bushes, and trees. A little bush of brown grass-like reeds drew my attention. Suddenly it moved, even though there was no breeze, and I realized that even though it looked like a normal part of nature, it was the hair on top of the head of a troll-like creature. At that point the creature jumped out of the earth and started running in circles. I knew I was the only one who had noticed it, since no one else paid it any attention. Plus, it hadn't taken on full physical form and was slightly translucent. Even though I could see it with my eyes, it seemed to exist in the realm between our physical world and the dream world. It ran round in circles a few times without noticing me or paying attention to anyone else, and then disappeared into thin air. This surprised me, since I hadn't expected to see a nature spirit right in the middle of such a busy place.

That same summer in Barcelona, I went for a walk in a public park, but this time I intended to connect with a nature spirit. I climbed a tree to meditate and put myself in the right state of mind. Then I started scanning the bark of the tree. After a few minutes, a small round face emerged, opened its eyes, looked at me, and disappeared again. I smiled, because my experiment had worked. I'd recreated an experience I'd had years earlier, when I'd seen a similar face pop out from a leaf of one of my pot plants in my apartment in Berlin.

These and similar experiences taught me that the trick to seeing nature spirits is two-fold. First, you need to realize that each plant, tree, and stone is a living being in its own right and has a spirit that can manifest in our 3D world. Secondly, it's important to relax your eyes and let your vision become blurry. Then look at the plant, bush, or tree as if you were trying to see shapes in the clouds. This allows nature spirits to break through our preconceived notions of our natural environment and appear to us.

What exactly are nature spirits?

Nature spirits are spirits of the natural world who live in the same space we live in but on a different frequency. They're responsible for giving our environment its shape by turning pure energy into physical matter. Each culture and spiritual tradition has its own names for them and distinguishes different types. Most acknowledge those connected to the elements, like water spirits, air spirits, earth spirits, and fire spirits. There are also spirits who inhabit certain mountains, trees, rivers, or other natural features that are important or stand out to the local human population. And of course, all cultures recognize Mother Earth herself as a sentient being. This means that the spirits of the moon, the sun, the planets, and the stars are also nature spirits and can communicate with us.

My personal understanding is that each manifestation of nature, be it a rose, a cloud, or a mushroom, has its own spirit, just as each human has a soul connected to an Earthly body. This means each blade of grass and each drop of rainwater has a consciousness that our senses can perceive as a nature spirit. These individual spirits can work together and form a bigger entity with its own consciousness, in a similar way to how our individual cells make up our body. So, we can communicate with individual rocks or an entire mountain and learn different lessons from each.

Yes, nature spirits can teach us, but they aren't all friendly toward humans. This shouldn't be a surprise. As you can imagine, the nature spirits that inhabit places that have been exploited and abused by humans don't count us among their friends, and can even be hostile toward us and try to shoo us away. So it's important to distinguish between the nature spirits who want to act as our guides and the ones who don't. The ones who do will enlist our help in restoring the balance between humans and nature and healing the environment. So, if you want to attract a nature spirit, pick up some trash in your local park while you walk your dog. You could even enlist the help of your neighbors and make it a community event. Consider your impact on nature and you'll make new friends among this type of spirit guide.

The fact that nature spirits are great at manifesting means that they can help us manifest what we want to create, as long as it serves the highest good of all. So they might not help you get a Ferrari, but they'll be happy to help you buy a more environmentally friendly car. You could also ask for the money to support a non-profit organization that protects the Amazon or start a business that creates sustainable fashion. Whatever your dreams and goals, ask for nature spirits' support and they'll teach you to use the laws of manifestation to achieve them. However, they'll ask for something in return, so think about how you can support them in exchange.

What also sets nature spirits apart from the other types of spirit guide is their healing ability. When I do spirit guide readings for clients who are healers, it's often nature spirits who are accompanying them. Their messages revolve around the healing properties of plants and herbs. They also encourage my clients to learn to exchange energy with plants without killing or eating them. Just sitting with a plant or herb and asking it for help can produce amazing results. This requires a radical new way of thinking, but nature spirits are here to help us through this change.

Guide characteristics

These guides are special because they live in a dimension that's very close to our own. Therefore, they can relate to us in a way that other types of guide can't. They're also closer to Mother Earth than most other guides (except animal spirits), which has a big influence on their characteristics.

Playful creativity

The first characteristic of nature spirits I want to discuss is their playful creativity. It shows up when they think you could use a good laugh. Once, when I wasn't feeling great, my bedroom wall lit up as if I'd turned on a projector screen. A group of elves appeared on it, danced around, and pulled funny faces at me. There was nothing I could do but laugh.

Nature spirits love life and enjoy having a good time. They remind us we aren't here to suffer. Instead, they want us to open up to the beauty and wonder of Planet Earth and savor all that life has to offer us.

Their playfulness also results in boundless creativity, imagination, and originality. Nature itself reflects this in so many beautiful ways. There's such a wide variety of plants, flowers, and trees all around us. Where does all this diversity come from? It's the work of fun-loving and inventive nature spirits.

Manifestation skills

The second characteristic you should know about is nature spirits' amazing talent to translate an idea or dream into physical reality. They possess these extraordinary manifesting skills because they're the ones that give shape to the woods, oceans, mountains, plants, and trees that make up Mother Earth, and they're happy to help us develop manifestation skills ourselves. We might not conjure our dream house or a new car out of thin air. However, if we invest the time and energy needed, we can create a happy, fulfilling, and rewarding life for ourselves and others that goes beyond anything we can imagine.

In contrast to some humans, companies, and governments, nature spirits work *with* Mother Earth to create the best solution for all beings involved. This results in better outcomes and is a much easier way for us to manifest our dream life than working against the natural laws of our planet and the highest good of all. One of the highest priorities of nature spirits is to share their wisdom and extraordinary manifesting skills to bring balance and co-operation between all living beings here on our beautiful planet.

The ability to heal the physical world

Because nature spirits created so much of what we see here on our planet, they can also fix and heal anything broken or out of alignment. This includes our natural environment and our physical body. These spirits know exactly which herbs we should take, which crystals we should use, and which rituals we should conduct to restore balance. They love working with herbalists, crystal therapists, animal communicators, and other people who make it their mission to heal others with the help of plants, herbs, and other natural means. They love any kind of natural healing modality and want to encourage us to add these to our own health regime. If you listen to them, they'll encourage you to stay in great shape and heal any issues you might face in a natural way.

They're also at the forefront of saving our planet from the destruction it's facing. And they're looking for humans who can assist them. If a nature spirit guide is working with you, one reason for it is that you have the potential to further this cause.

Gifts

A nature spirit guide brings gifts that can serve us in more than just one way. They can bring us more joy and ease by helping us discover our lightheartedness. Another gift is their ability to bring us closer to our animal companions and open us up to the reality that all animals are our brothers and sisters. They also gift us with practical magic that we can apply in our daily lives to achieve the goals we've set for ourselves.

Lightheartedness

The first gift nature spirits can bring us is a more cheerful outlook on life. Do you focus more on the things you fear, avoid, and worry about than on the possibilities, opportunities, and blessings in front of you? If so, you can definitely benefit from the lightheartedness that nature spirits bring.

At the core of their optimistic viewpoint lies trust in life, the Universe, and self. This can be difficult for us if our natural faith has taken serious hits from trauma during childhood and beyond. We need to recognize that the Universe isn't working against us or punishing us. Once we understand this, we can release the need to control everything and stop making life harder than it has to be. Nature spirits can help us heal and get back to a more balanced and high-spirited existence. Then our heart will feel lighter and we can enjoy the incarnation experience to its fullest.

A strong bond with animals

Nature spirits live in close proximity to the animals that roam this planet. They're the true caretakers of Mother Earth. They mold the surface of our planet and give it shape. However, they don't do so just for their own benefit, but take the needs of the animals (including us) into consideration at all times. Even though not all humans can detect their presence, animals can. Have you ever seen your pet stare into a bush or up a tree and not been able to figure out why? They may have sensed the presence of a nature spirit!

This type of spirit guide opens us up to the reality that we humans aren't the center of the Universe and are just one life form among many. We don't have special privileges and are no more important than a dog, a cow, or a slug. This insight is the gift that allows us to create a strong bond with the other animals and, therefore, build a better world for all beings on Earth.

A natural talent for magic

The third gift we can unlock if we have a nature spirit as a cosmic guide is magic. Yes, you heard that right. Magic is real. Even though we can't go beyond the laws of physics, we *can* magic into existence almost everything our heart desires, no matter what our starting point is. The trick is careful planning and execution. Yes, we have to invest time and energy. But that doesn't make it less magical that we can alter reality and create a better life for ourselves and others.

As long as we're working for the highest good of all, nature spirits are happy to share their natural talent for magic with us. We can then share in the responsibility and joy of creating a more inclusive, egalitarian, and collaborative future. All we need to do is be open to our own unique gifts, skills, and talents, because these are the key to our magical abilities.

Challenges

Besides the characteristics and gifts already discussed, nature spirits also come with their own set of challenges. This shouldn't dissuade you from working with them. In fact, knowing about these pitfalls enables you to avoid them and enjoy your relationship with nature spirits even more.

Lack of discipline

The first challenge comes from the fact that nature spirits like to enjoy themselves. They're playful and love to spend their time relaxing and planning fun parties. This works out great for them, but if we do the same and lose our sense of discipline, we'll suffer the negative consequences down the road. As human beings, we need to take daily action to manifest our dreams.

Fortunately, our nature spirit guides can help with that; they don't want us to spend all our time on mindless entertainment. As already mentioned, they're great at manifesting and can teach us to do it for ourselves. And we can have fun doing it! No one said it needs to be a somber affair. However, don't forget that in our dimension it's important to work with the physical realities of life. Projects like starting your own business or moving to another country take discipline. But your nature spirit guide will be eager to add some magic to your efforts.

Losing orientation in life

There are many stories about nature spirits luring humans into the woods or hollow hills to attend one of their famous parties, complete with music, dance, and mind-altering beverages. Once the event ends and the human goes back home, they discover that not just a few hours have passed, but years or even decades.

I've never met anyone this has literally happened to, but I can attest to the fact that nature spirits can disorient some people on a more subtle level. This isn't because they're evil. It happens because they live in a dimension that's similar to ours but not the same. If we spend too much time in their world and not enough grounded in our own, we can become lost on an emotional level. Nature spirits who act as our guides know of this danger and prevent it by inviting us to stay grounded at all times. They also encourage us to be present in our own lives instead of letting our souls flee into a world that isn't our own.

Anger about the destruction of our environment

As nature spirits are the true keepers of Mother Earth, it's no wonder they get upset when they witness us treating our planet as a commodity and an exploitable resource. If you work with this type of spirit guide, it's likely that you have similar concerns and also get upset when you see others disrespecting Mother Nature.

Even though this can be a challenge sometimes, it's also a clear sign that it's part of your purpose to raise awareness of the destruction of the environment or even take action to demand respect for our planet. You don't have to chain yourself to a tree to prevent others from cutting it down (unless you want to); there are myriad ways to help solve our current environmental problems. Your spirit guide encourages you to make a difference wherever you can, be it by educating your children about this issue, reminding your friends to discard their trash responsibly, or donating to a good cause.

What does your connection to a nature spirit say about you?

Let's talk about some of the personality traits of people who feel drawn to work with nature spirits, since there are some commonalities. You might or might not recognize these attributes and qualities in yourself. However, if you look back over your life, you'll discover that you had them all along. Now it's time to start working with them.

You have a natural sense for power places and ley lines

Both you and your nature spirit guide have a love for Mother Earth and can sense her subtle electrical currents when they form power places and ley lines. The former are like our chakras – energy centers where several currents meet – and regulate certain functions of the planet. The latter are like our meridian system, a network of channels through which our life energy, in Chinese medicine known as *chi*, flows. They span the globe and allow energies to flow from one power place to the next. Together, ley lines and power places form the energy grid of our planet.

You might not know that you can sense these energy points and lines. Like many spiritual abilities, it can feel so normal to you that you don't realize that not everyone experiences life the way you do. But to work with this energy grid, you first need to become conscious of it. Go for a walk in nature or a park and pay attention to the energy in different places. How does it feel? Ask your guide to help and you'll soon be able to use your sense for power places and ley lines to serve your life purpose.

You make an excellent peaceful warrior for the environment

As nature spirits act as the guardians of Mother Earth, they don't condone the violence and suffering we humans inflict on our planet and its non-human inhabitants. The same is true for you. Visiting a beach covered with washed-up trash saddens you and knowing that the Amazon rainforest is becoming smaller by the day can fill you with anger. And rightly so! Use that fire in your belly to collaborate with your guide, take action, and make a difference in this world. Organize a neighborhood initiative to clean up your street or local park, raise awareness on social media, or donate to an environmental cause. Whatever you do, do *something*. Being a caretaker for nature is at least part of your purpose here on Earth, otherwise you wouldn't be working with a nature spirit.

Your spiritual view of life and your nature spirit guide will help you find peaceful ways to create positive change, either through one big effort or small baby steps. Whatever form your path takes, know that every tiny effort helps and your guide appreciates it very much.

You're a natural healer

Your sensitivity to the energies of Mother Earth makes you an excellent healer. You share this trait with people who work with angels. However, whereas they do their work on an emotional level, you heal with plants, herbs, and crystals. If you've ever had to battle with health issues, your spirit guide will have led you to explore alternative methods like herbal medicine, crystal therapy, homeopathy, sacred plant medicines, and more. The ancient techniques of shamanic healing fascinate you, and for good reason. They rely on the healing tools that Mother Earth provides and they call us to heal ourselves and others.

Don't worry, you don't have to move to the Amazon or become a professional crystal healer if you don't want to. Just experiment on yourself to see if you can heal your own aches and pains. Then use what you've learnt to help family and friends whenever they're in need. If you want to take it to the next level, you can then see clients. Though always make sure that your patient, be it yourself or someone else, coordinates your efforts with their physician!

Nature spirit communication around the world

Nature spirits have been known by many names across the globe and through the centuries, from the friendly Aziza in the African kingdom of Dahomey, who provided game for hunters, to the beautiful Greek nymphs, who made the gods fall in love with them, to the capricious English fairies, who danced in the woods. In many cultures, offerings are one way to communicate with them. From the Buryat in Mongolia to the Emberá in Colombia and the San people in South Africa, there's the belief that leaving little gifts out for nature spirits shows that you're seriously seeking to connect with them. Picking the right offering also confirms that you're bringing something of yourself to the table. Nature spirits value reciprocity, since it's one of the cornerstone laws of our physical dimension. Offerings can be different according to location and tradition. Traditional gifts include milk, honey, nuts, coins, crystals, prayers, dance, or even a song (remember, nature spirits enjoy creative expression). In our day and age, an excellent method of honoring nature spirits is to invest your time and energy in keeping the planet clean. Collecting trash while out for a walk is a great offering!

Another method of connecting with nature spirits is co-creating your backyard, porch, or balcony with them. The Findhorn Foundation is a community in Scotland founded by Peter and Eileen Caddy and Dorothy Maclean in the 60s. They started growing vegetables with the help of the local nature spirits, which they called Devas ('divine beings' in Hindi). This resulted in plants that grew faster and bigger than most would, especially in the sandy soil of the area. Astounded horticultural experts came to visit. Soon Findhorn developed into a thriving community of people exploring ways of living in harmony with nature.

Traditional spirit workers and contemporary Western seekers who work with nature spirits often connect with them outside in nature. First they go out to find their dwelling places (often unusual vegetation or rock formations). Then they go into a light trance to shift their mind into the dimension these beings reside in. Finally they ask for the help they need. This could be information on the right plants or herbs to use in a healing ceremony, the best place to build a house, or how to get food on the table.

There's sometimes a historical connection between a nature spirit and a family lineage, as with the Lébou people in Senegal and their Tuur spirits. The connection is built over generations with regular offerings and altars to the nature spirits. We may even have such a connection ourselves, though we're unaware of it. I've had a few clients whose nature spirit guides told us they had worked with their ancestral lineage before.

Receiving the call

Spirit workers throughout history and across the world who have had a nature spirit as one of their spirit guides have received the call to work with them in the following ways:

- a deep love of a distinct locale in nature or the planet as a whole

- feeling a presence when outdoors, especially in specific places

- dreams of elves, fairies, and other elementals

- an ancestral connection to a specific nature spirit or spirits

It's up to you to create a unique communication style to use to converse with your nature spirit guide. Review what you learnt in this chapter. Which parts resonated with you on an intuitive level? Which parts didn't make much sense to you? And what would you like to try or learn more about? If you wish, you can make notes in your workbook (*see Bonuses, p.243*), ready for when you get to create your own ritual to connect with the specific nature spirit you're working with.

NATURE SPIRITS AT A GLANCE

Characteristics: Playful creativity, manifestation skills, the ability to heal the physical world (including our bodies and the environment)

Gifts: Lightheartedness, a strong bond with animals, a natural talent for magic

Challenges: Lack of discipline, losing orientation in life, anger about the destruction of our environment

What having this type of spirit guide says about you: You have a natural sense for power places and ley lines, you make an excellent peaceful warrior for the environment; you're a natural healer.

Next, we'll look at animal guides – their characteristics, gifts, and challenges, what having one as a spirit guide says about you, and how humans have worked with them throughout history and across cultures.

~

CHAPTER 8

ANIMAL GUIDES

I'd just meditated for 30 minutes, as always before doing a spirit guide reading, and I was ready. My candle was lit, and I opened my laptop to meet my client and give her any messages her guides might have for her. When she came online, the energy in the room shot up and I realized this would be a special session. The first 15 minutes, during which I told her about the spirit guides that came forward to speak to her, proceeded as usual. Then, *my* healing guide, Grandfather Bear, popped in and asked me to do a healing on my client by singing a specific melody he uses to transfer energy. I told her about this and she agreed to go along with this sudden change of plan.

After singing for just a few seconds, I heard weird clicking and banging noises. I kept my eyes closed, as I always do for better focus, and proceeded with the healing, but the noises kept getting louder and more distinct and suddenly my client spoke in a deep, guttural voice. It was impossible that a human voice box could produce such sounds. Surprised, I opened my eyes and realized my client had fallen into a trance and was channeling another being! This had never happened before and it took me a second to compose myself. Grandfather Bear advised me to keep going, so I did. Then the entity speaking through my client said a few sentences in what sounded to me like an ancient language I couldn't understand.

Now, two years later, I still don't have a satisfying explanation for what transpired during that reading. But that doesn't matter. What counts is that Grandfather Bear, an animal spirit, facilitated a healing for my client, which she thanked me for later, and it was an unforgettable experience for me. It inspired me to learn more about trance states and how spirit workers across cultures have used them to retrieve information from the spirit world. I suspect that was the point for me!

The first time I met Grandfather Bear was during my time at university in Germany. I was going through a rough time because it didn't feel as though my studies were helping me create the future I desired. Struggling to define *what* I wanted in life, I sensed a calling deep down in my heart, but I didn't understand what it meant. I tried resisting it, even though it wouldn't leave me alone. It invited me to read everything I could about spirituality, otherworldly encounters, and Neo-Shamanism.

At the same time, I was having multiple visions and dreams that were showing me that a spirit entity wished to enter my life. In these visions I kept seeing two different beings, a bear and an older Native American man who, judging by his regalia, was a healer from the Great Plains. However, I was still very inexperienced at communicating with spirits and asked myself if I was just imagining things or if I'd gone mad.

One morning, I woke up from a dream that brought some clarity. In it, I'd seen the bear transform into the Native American man and back again. I now realized they were the same spirit guide showing itself to me in two different forms. Over time, I'd also come to recognize that the visions I'd had of Grandfather Bear were always connected to the theme of healing. The reason he'd showed himself as an indigenous healer was because I'd been reading so much about Neo-Shamanism. He'd used my frame of reference to convey the message that he was my healer guide.

What exactly are animal guides?

Defining animal guides is a difficult task, because many people around the world have similar concepts but use different terms and definitions. Some cultures in South America, like the Emberá in Colombia, call them the Mothers, Fathers, Lords, or Masters of a specific animal species. Examples are the Mother of Fish and the Master of Jaguars. The Anishinaabe, several culturally related indigenous peoples in the Pacific Northwest of the United States and Canada, have 'totem animals.' These are the spirits of an animal species related to a group of people like a family, clan, or lineage. In some Neo-Pagan traditions, we find the term 'familiars,' which derives from medieval European folklore and describes animal guides who assist witches in practicing their magic. You might also come across the term 'power animal' as used by the Neo-Shamanic tradition taught by modern teachers like Michael Harner and

Sandra Ingerman. In addition, we find the term 'spirit animal.' The latter gets misused a lot on the Internet to define a person, animal, or thing that we admire and are inspired by. To avoid the pitfall of cultural appropriation, I don't use any of the aforementioned names. I recommend you don't either, unless you're a member of that specific culture or spiritual tradition.

Instead, we need a term to describe the relationship that serious spiritual seekers who aren't part of a specific culture or spiritual tradition have with this type of spirit guide. I opt to call them 'animal guides.' I understand it as a general term for spirit guides who appear in animal form and represent the collective spirit of a specific animal species. They act as guardians, mentors, teachers, and companions. We shouldn't confuse them with the spirit of an individual animal that's passed. Shared characteristics like sensitivity and resourcefulness connect us with them, as well as regular personal experience and interaction with their Earthly counterparts, or shared talents, skills, and gifts. Totem animals, power animals, familiars, spirit animals, and other specific cultural definitions could fall under this umbrella. However, I'll leave it to the people in the cultures and traditions that use those terms to define that for themselves. The rest of us who feel that our lives are guided by this type of spirit guide and have authentic experiences with them can use the term 'animal guide.'

One distinct form of animal guide that I want to mention is the therianthrope. This is a shapeshifter who transforms from human into animal form and vice versa or is both at the same time. The name comes from the Greek *therion*, meaning 'wild animal,' and *anthropos*, meaning 'human.' Cave paintings of such beings reach back to Paleolithic times and exist on almost all continents, suggesting that we've worked with them for a very long time. Nowadays, the best-known forms of therianthropes are werewolves, centaurs, and mermaids. Other common combinations are half-human with the other half being a bear, a feline, a stag, a bird, or a dog. We sometimes classify them as gods rather than animal guides, as is the case with Anubis, the Egyptian deity with a human body and the head of a canine. This shows again that classifying animal guides can be tricky. Not all therianthropes are friendly toward humans, so most don't work with us as spirit guides. Those who do make powerful spirit guides because they're so ancient and related to humanity and its evolution.

As you can see, animal guides have a long history. They come in many shapes, forms, and sizes, but with distinct characteristics, gifts, and challenges. Let's discuss these now, along with how people have connected with animal guides across cultures and history.

Guide characteristics

There are many kinds of animal roaming our beautiful planet, and there's just as much diversity with animal guides in the spirit world. They come in all shapes and sizes and with different personalities and attributes. The fierceness of a lion is a far shot from the industriousness of an ant. Still, there are some general characteristics that all animal guides have in common. Let's look at these now.

A strong connection to Mother Earth

Since animals are children of the Earth, animal guides have a strong connection to this planet. They're born from the womb of her spirit, just as their living counterparts are born from her physical body. They often come through in my spirit guide readings when a client's soul needs more grounding to express itself fully here on the physical plane. They help bring us down to earth if we spend too much time in our head. They also make us feel safe again on the Earth plane if a traumatic event is keeping us stuck in fear and escapism. They often recommend walking barefoot on the earth and spending as much time as possible in nature to facilitate a stronger connection to the planet. Sometimes they want us to connect to a specific place that can help us heal and align with our true selves. This helps us to be present instead of reliving the past or worrying about the future.

Playful humor

All spirit guides sometimes use humor to teach us important lessons, and animal guides are the most hilarious by far. They're very playful and like to provide some comic relief after a serious message. They encourage us to follow their lead and laugh more, enjoy life, and bring out our inner child from time to time. This doesn't mean they're silly or that we shouldn't take them seriously; they just complement their deep insights with a joyous, sometimes tongue-in-cheek humor that helps us to lighten up. In my experience, animal guides will sometimes even come through as a younger version of themselves, as it's easy for us to open our hearts to a kitten, a puppy, or a baby dolphin, and therefore accept their message. They also understand that having fun while manifesting our dreams and goals is one of the best ways to achieve the results we're after. They don't allow us to get stuck by overthinking things.

Easy to relate and connect to

Because of their close connection to Mother Earth through their physical counterparts, animal guides know what life on this planet is like. They not only know the restrictions, but also the joy that comes with being incarnated. This makes them easy to relate to. There isn't a big gap in consciousness between us, as is the case with an angel or a star being. Therefore, their guidance is often more practical and applicable than that of some of the other types of guide. They're concerned with our day-to-day lives, providing for ourselves and our families, and developing our human selves to become the best we can be.

Because they're so close to our human dimension, it's easy to connect to animal guides. Their energy and characteristics are close to our own and easy to pick up on. If you're having difficulty communicating with any of the other types of guide, try connecting with an animal guide first. Yes, ancestor guides are even closer to us. However, shared karma and unresolved emotions connected to our forefathers can make it difficult for our ego to tell the difference between what we want (or fear) to hear and a real message. There's no such problem with animal guides.

Gifts

The blessings given to us by the animal guides that accompany us through life are great opportunities to enrich our experience as a physical being. The tribulations of life are easier to endure with the gifts our animal guides bring us. They provide us with the skills to use our environment to align ourselves with our own inner nature. They make us feel welcome and at home here in the physical realm, and connect us with the wisdom of our body.

Alignment with our inner nature

We've already discussed animal guides' strong connection to Mother Earth, but here I want to share a related gift that can enrich your life. Working with an animal guide invites us to immerse ourselves in the natural world so we can also align ourselves with our inner nature. The more time we spend communing with nature, the more our soul has the chance to express itself naturally. The artificial expressions of ourselves that we use to survive in our high-pressured societies fall away to make room for just *being*.

This doesn't mean you have to become a camping fanatic, it just means that observing the natural environment around you, be it in the middle of a hectic city or in the peace of a national park, brings you back to yourself. It's great for when you're indecisive, insecure, or stuck. Just touch the bark of a tree for a few minutes and focus on the energy flowing up and down its trunk. It can help regulate your own energy flow and bring you back into balance. Another example is watching the clouds pass by, reminding you that your stressful thoughts are just temporary.

Protection

Another gift animal guides bring with them is protection. We instinctively know this, so we prefer a guide that's strong, like a wolf, a bear, or a tiger. When we discover that the animal spirit that's accompanying us through life is a smaller, non-aggressive, and unimpressive animal, it sometimes disappoints us. However, even the tiniest representative of this type of spirit guide can teach us important lessons about how to protect ourselves.

When I was living in Berlin, there was a summer when there were thousands of slugs in the park I used to go to. They were everywhere! Even though most people found them ugly and gross, I befriended them because I realized how brave they were to incarnate into such soft and sensitive bodies, with no way to flee or protect themselves from the harsh reality of this world. I made sure never to step on them and saved a lot of them from being run over by cars. In return, the spirit of slug spoke to me one day and taught me that I was highly sensitive too, and that I needed to practice psychic protection daily to shield my energy field, function better in daily life and hone my sensitivity instead of getting overwhelmed by it. I'll forever be grateful for this lesson, because it changed my life. Now, imagine I hadn't paid attention to this animal guide because a slug wasn't the spirit guide I'd envisioned for myself... Protection can come in many forms. Every animal guide has its own way of providing it for us.

Enhanced instincts

An instinct is an automatic reaction to a certain stimulus. One example is the fight-or-flight response. No one has taught us how to do it and we don't go through a decision-making process either, we just do it. We smile when we're happy. We hold our breath under water. Our hormones react when we find someone attractive. These instincts and many more are our subconscious reactions to life. If we didn't have them, we'd be in a constant state of analysis paralysis.

Animal guides can gift us with enhanced instincts. This doesn't mean that we act on autopilot and our subconscious makes all the decisions. What it does mean is that, depending on the animal spirit we're working with, we react faster and with more certainty in specific areas of our life. Here is an example from my own life. When I do a reading for a client and Grandfather Bear shows up, I don't just know that the client needs a healing, I instinctively know what I need to do. I don't weigh all the options first, I just know and act on that knowledge.

Challenges

Working with spirit guides isn't all rainbows and unicorns, and working with animal guides is no exception. They come with their own set of challenges that we need to consider and deal with. Here are the three most important issues you'll encounter when working with animal guides.

Acting before thinking things through

The enhanced instincts animal guides bring can be a great blessing. However, if we become impulsive and immediately act on anything that bubbles up from the deep well of our psyche without thinking things through, we can get into serious trouble, from accidents to broken relationships. Our subconscious can be a treasure trove, but also contains a lot of raw thoughts and emotions. We need to process these before projecting them into the world through instinctive actions.

To avoid this pitfall, animal spirits will guide us into situations that assist us in slowing down and assessing the situation before acting. So, if you're in a situation where your instinctive reactions threaten to take over, pause. Realize this is a chance for you to rewire your brain and create new behavioral patterns that include calmness, self-control, and deliberation.

Competitiveness

Experience has taught us all that the world is a competitive place. Competition is everywhere – in sibling rivalry, sports games, the workplace, politics, and international relations. When we observe animals, we also witness fierce competition when resources or mating partners are scarce. There's nothing wrong with this. A healthy sense of competition keeps us on our toes and helps us set bigger goals. However, when collaboration becomes impossible because our main goal is to best everyone else, it doesn't serve our best interests anymore.

Working with an animal guide can sometimes trigger this behavior. Not because the guide wants us to be that way, but because we over-identify with our guides and forget to consider our own human-based wisdom. Only if we consult and listen to ourselves first and then ask for guidance from the spirit world can we become the best version of ourselves. If we make our animal guide responsible for our happiness, we'll fail. Their animal responses aren't suitable to lead us to happiness. They know that and therefore won't answer any and every question we might have for them. Like any good teacher, they encourage us to figure things out for ourselves first.

Physical sensitivity

The third challenge we can encounter when working with animal guides is down to the fact that our body is highly sensitive. It's affected by energies from other people, non-physical beings, and places. This is actually a great gift, since it means our body can function as a finely tuned instrument and help us perceive and interpret our environment and interactions with others. Maybe you can tell if someone is in a bad mood because you can feel it in your stomach. Or you can even sense other people's aches and pains in your own body. But it becomes a problem if we're unaware of this dynamic. Therefore, our guide wants us to be mindful of our Earthly vehicle, eat healthily, create strong psychic boundaries, and flush out any energies that aren't helpful. Health issues such as allergies can be a sign we're dealing with this challenge.

Our physical sensitivity mirrors that of our animal spirit. Animal spirit guides are non-physical beings, but their worldly counterparts are very attuned to the physical plane and their bodies. It's our job to be the same, pay attention to what our body is telling us, and act accordingly.

What does your connection to an animal guide say about you?

Besides the gifts and challenges that come with an animal guide, having this type of celestial helper can also tell you a lot about your own personality. Here are three characteristics that people working with animal guides have in common.

You're protective of family and community

If you have an animal spirit guide, your loved ones feel safe around you because you're protective of them and would never let anything bad happen to them. This is true for your direct family members, your circle of close friends, and sometimes your entire community. Environmental activists, for instance, often work with animal guides. They dedicate their lives to protecting not just their human relatives, but also the non-human ones, like animals, plants, trees, and rocks.

Even if you'd never classify yourself as a family person, the people who are important to you can attest to your loyalty. When you realize that someone is mistreating them, you get upset and get the urge to do something about it. You're like a big brother or sister who comes to the rescue. It depends on the rest of your personality if you roar like a lion in their enemy's face or annoy the heck out of them like a tiny mosquito. But either way, you do whatever it takes to make sure they're safe.

You're physically oriented

If one of your main guides is an animal spirit, this also shows you're a physically oriented person. This doesn't mean you're a top athlete or a supermodel, but it does mean your body is your partner and you want to work with it and pay it special attention. We've already mentioned that our physical sensitivity can be a challenge (and a gift!) and I want to expand on this, because it's an often overlooked but important aspect of ourselves.

With an animal spirit guide, your physical orientation shows you gather information from your 3D environment, love working with physical tools like tarot cards and crystals to gain spiritual information, and have strong 'gut feelings.' You love adorning your body with jewelry and nice clothes. You're also very creative, be it as an artist, interior designer, florist, or hobby knitter. Your communication style includes touch and lots of hugs to get your point across. With spirit guide communication, you might even have experienced some physical manifestations like inexplicable sounds around the house, moving objects, or one of your guides appearing in physical form.

You're strongly connected to the natural environment

One more characteristic people with animal guides have in common is a strong connection to the natural environment. This means you need to connect with nature to stay healthy and balanced. Putting your naked feet on the earth or in water calms you down, re-energizes you, and brings you back into your body. An open window at night helps you get a good night's sleep. And living in a place that allows you to connect with Mother Earth is essential for your happiness. This strong connection to nature can also be the initial impulse or experience that sets you on your spiritual path.

When I was a child, I loved going for walks in the woods behind our house. I'd let my intuition lead me and often end up in places that felt special to me. I couldn't put words to the sensation. All I knew was that it felt sacred, just like entering a church or temple.

Animal guide communication across cultures

We've already seen that animal guides are very common across the entire globe. However, there are big differences in how people define, describe, and perceive them. Every culture or spiritual tradition uses different names to identify them and has developed individual ways to connect with them.

The famous Paleolithic cave paintings in Lascaux, France, are some of the first recorded human-made images of animals and are said to have a ritualistic and spiritual meaning. They're similar to the spiritual art of the San people (also known as the !Kung) in southern Africa, which depicts animal guides like the eland. We don't know how the people in the Lascaux valley connected with their animal guides, but the San shamans dance for hours at a time to rhythmic clapping and singing by the women. They then slip into a trance state, which enables them to have out-of-body experiences and travel to the spirit world. This is when they can take on the potency and power of a particular animal guide like the eland or giraffe and use it for healing.

Nowadays, some pagans and Wiccans work with what they call 'familiars.' These assist them in their practice of magic as servants and messengers. The concept of the familiar spirit is hundreds of years old and originated in Britain. Familiars were said to have supernatural powers, which was a reason for the Inquisition to associate them with the devil and burn their owners as witches. Even the animals themselves were often tried, convicted, and murdered. The black cat is the classic example of a familiar, but dogs, toads, ravens, and other creatures are also said to take on that role. What makes the familiar stand apart from other types of animal guide is the fact that they're actual incarnated animals. Most other types are non-physical entities. Familiars can either spontaneously appear to us or come as an inheritance from family members or teachers. Sometimes our main spirit guide can introduce them to us, or we can acquire them while going through a difficult time like an illness or trauma.

Another form of animal guide you might be familiar with is the power animal of Neo-Shamanism. Michael Harner popularized this concept in his book *The Way of the Shaman*. Many spiritual seekers have learnt his technique for acquiring and communicating with power animals. It's a form of guided meditation accompanied by drumming (live or recorded). It leads the spiritual seeker to the underworld via a hole in the ground, a cave, a hollow tree, or a similar entrance that ends in a tunnel. This brings them to the lowest of the three levels of the spirit world, where the power animals reside. Here, the guided part of the meditation stops and the traveler gets to experience the encounter without further guidance. Quickening of the drumming shows when it's time to return to the ordinary world of human beings.

Receiving the call

Spirit workers throughout history and across the world who have had an animal guide as one of their spirit guides have received the call to work with them in the following ways:

- regular, real-life encounters with a physical representative of an animal guide

- a fascination with one of the spiritual traditions that work with animal guides

- an ancestral connection to a specific animal guide

- repeated synchronicities that involve an animal guide

- dreams that feature this type of guide

As you can see from even this small collection of examples, each culture and spiritual tradition has its own way of connecting and communicating with animal guides. It's up to you to create a unique communication style to converse with your animal guide. Consider what you learnt in this chapter. Which parts resonated with you on an intuitive level? Which parts didn't make much sense to you? And what would you like to try or learn more about? If you wish, you can make notes in your workbook (*see Bonuses, p.243*), ready for when you get to create your own ritual to connect with the specific animal guide you're working with.

ANIMAL GUIDES AT A GLANCE

Characteristics: A strong connection to Mother Earth, playful humor, easy to relate and connect to

Gifts: Alignment with our inner nature, protection, enhanced instincts

Challenges: Acting before thinking things through, competitiveness, physical sensitivity

What having this type of spirit guide says about you: You're protective of family and community, physically oriented, and strongly connected to the natural environment.

Next, we'll look at star beings – their characteristics, gifts, and challenges, what having one as a spirit guide says about you, and how humans have worked with them throughout history and across cultures.

~

CHAPTER 9

STAR BEINGS

I looked up and saw them – three star beings, in my bedroom in Berlin, in the middle of the night. Looking just like the grays in the movies, with big heads, large, dark almond-shaped eyes, and long, spindly arms and legs. Two stood close to the door. One was kneeling as if about to ask someone to marry him. I'd just got out of bed to head into the hallway. We stared at each other. They seemed surprised that I could see them and froze for a second. Once they had recovered from the shock, one of them shot over to me and touched my wrist. It wasn't threatening and it happened so quickly that there was no chance to get scared. I don't remember what happened next.

When I woke up the next morning, there was no sign of them. My partner at the time was still sound asleep next to me. Nothing seemed out of the ordinary. Still, I realized the experience hadn't been a dream but a real alien encounter! I had no doubt about it.

Even though they never appeared again, those beings taught me an important lesson that night. Once I was fully awake the next morning, I had a big insight: I realized that my physical body had never left my bed. It was my astral body that had got up to wander the Universe and made the surprising discovery. This was astonishing news, since I hadn't thought it was possible to astral travel without remembering it. But we do it more often than we realize.

This encounter also gave me direct experience of how the so-called silver cord works. I knew this etheric string connected the astral body with the physical body and pulled the traveling astral body back into the physical body if the body felt in danger. It's for this reason that we should never touch a person in a trance or even in a meditation: the body will automatically go into alarm mode and bring the wandering spirit back, which can be quite a jarring experience. That's exactly what the star being had done: it had touched my wrist because it knew that my astral self would retreat into my physical body and I'd forget about the beings' presence.

I wasn't interested in aliens when I was younger. I always thought it unlikely that our planet was the only place in the Universe to bring forth life, but I didn't investigate further until I started dating someone interested in this topic, who introduced me to the books by Zecharia Sitchin. We also watched many movies about aliens and I discovered a worldwide community of people who identified as star beings incarnated in human bodies. It opened my mind to many new realities and led me to discover a love for the stars. Once I even witnessed a human transform into a star being in broad daylight.

During that time of new discoveries, I also started building my first online business. This was no coincidence, as I now know that many star beings are here to help humanity develop new technologies, including the Internet. I'm also convinced that many people who use the Internet for good have star beings as spirit guides. So, to connect with star beings, we needn't wait for them to visit us in physical form – we can always connect with them via telepathy, our inner 'technology.'

What exactly are star beings?

Here on Earth, we've studied the stars since the beginning of time. We've given them names, likened them to gods, depicted them in artwork, and tracked their movements across the sky to see how they influence our daily lives. Naturally, we've also wondered if there are other sentient beings out there, other life forms on other planets, star beings...

We often think of star beings as synonymous with aliens, but they aren't the same. I don't like to call them 'aliens' to avoid the negative stereotypes depicted in scary Hollywood movies. I don't want anyone to come to me for a spirit guide reading and get terrified when I tell them there's a star being guiding them. Yes, there are star beings who don't make great spirit guides because their objectives don't include our highest good. However, the ones who serve as guides throughout our lives are always well-meaning and trustworthy. I want my clients to know that it's a great honor to work with star beings. They bring many gifts and unique insights that go beyond the knowledge available on this planet right now.

If you work with a star being, you're a pioneer of some sort who is bringing new energies to Earth and creating the future as we speak.

Not all star beings resemble the typical grays I saw that night in my bedroom in Berlin. Just as there are many beings living on Earth, there are many beings living in the Universe – an infinite variety. Some possess a physical body, others don't. Some are humanoid, others aren't. Many have chosen developmental paths that are different from ours and our standard of measuring the success of a species doesn't apply to them. And, as mentioned when discussing nature spirits, there are also the spirits of the stars themselves who can connect with us.

Star beings are known all over the world. Look in the right places and you'll find them popping up throughout history in every corner of the globe. You can see them in eighteenth-century paintings like 'The Baptism of Christ' by Aert de Gelder, and in countless modern-day photos and videos. The most striking testimony to their existence is the fact that there are stories from every country imaginable about 'the ones that came from the stars' to teach, lead, and guide humanity. Stories of how they left us maps that depict our solar system looking from the outside in. Which explains why the Dogon in Mali knew about the rings of Saturn before Western scientists did. Others say that star beings gave us our culture or even created us. Nowadays, many think they came to prepare us to live in peace with one another and teach us how collaboration helps us to evolve.

To sum things up, the broad definition of star beings is 'any kind of life form that's not native to Mother Earth.' But here we'll work with a narrower definition, which only includes those star beings who have gone through the necessary soul development to serve as spirit guides.

Guide characteristics

Like the other six types of spirit guide, star beings aren't all the same. Each individual has its own personality, skills, and lessons to teach us. However, they all possess three characteristics that it's important to be aware of.

Cosmic consciousness

The first characteristic I want to talk about is the vast consciousness that star beings possess. Someone who is well traveled has witnessed first hand that, on the inside, all humans have the same needs and dreams. Star beings have a similar big-picture view of what unites living beings across the Universe. They realize that all sentient life forms come from the same source and share the same spark of light.

They also understand that once we humans come together to realize our true potential as a species, we can reach out to other species in different star systems and dimensions. Most of us aren't ready yet, but if you're working with a star being as a spirit guide, you're playing a role in making this a reality. Your guide will help you do this by expanding your mind and encouraging you to develop a vast, observational, and experiential mindset.

Able to harness energies

Another important characteristic of star beings is their knowledge of how to sense, manipulate, and harness universal energy. I often sense star beings around healers who help their clients shift energetic imbalances in their lives or physical bodies. However, you needn't be a healer to work with star beings. One of the biggest lessons anyone can learn from them is never to overuse their energy reserves, even if it's to help others. If we do drain ourselves in this way, we can't keep up with the work we set out to do. It's much better to think of the cosmos as a giant battery and let its energy flow through us. Star beings know just what kind of energy we need and where to find it. It might be in a faraway star system or a little pebble from our garden. Wherever it is, star beings will help us connect to it to reinforce our efforts, whether those involve healing ourselves or others, studying for an exam, running a marathon, or giving a talk in front of an audience.

An affinity for technology

Some of the most common star beings who serve as spirit guides are those who want to bring new technologies to humankind. They know that advances in science, communication, medicine, and so on help us move beyond the struggle for survival, which is what still preoccupies most people on this planet. Only when our mind is free of the need to find food and shelter can we go beyond fear and embrace peace and love. This will enable us to acknowledge that we're all one and that we need to unite to be stronger together. Just as each of us has an individual purpose, so humanity has one as a whole and we can only fulfill this together.

Star beings will help us achieve this, but the technology they bring isn't always the kind we might expect. It could look more like a new sewing pattern than the inside of a computer. According to Merriam-Webster, technology is 'the practical application of knowledge, especially in a particular area,' and whatever form it takes, the main thing is that it inspires you, and others, to connect with others.

Gifts

The Universe is vast and inhabited by many star beings, with many different characteristics, skills, personalities, and gifts. However, the ones who serve as spirit guides for humans have three specific gifts to share.

Energy healing

You might not be an official healer like a doctor, nurse, therapist, or Reiki master, but with a star being as a guide, you'll have the gift of energy healing. This will allow you to just sit with someone, doing nothing special, and they'll feel as if they've received an energy boost or an invisible force has made their burdens a little lighter. Your mere presence is healing. In fact, the more you try to make things happen and jump into frantic action to help others, the less successful you'll be. The trick is to let the universal forces use you as a channel so the healing energies can flow through you. All you need to do is move your ego out of the way. Let your guide do the rest. You can apply this strategy while healing yourself, other humans, animals, lakes, countries, or electrical appliances. Your star being will teach you how to do this. So let them take you by the hand and bring out this special gift that's slumbering inside your soul.

A healthy detachment from human drama

As humans, we're emotional creatures who can get caught up in the drama we create to numb ourselves, hide our little secrets, or avoid facing problems. We sometimes don't even realize how stuck we've become and that approaching a problem from a different perspective is what we need to move forward. Star beings have a more distant view of life on Earth and its challenges, and can therefore provide healthy detachment. Take this gift. Become an impassioned observer with a cool head. Disengage, let your spirit soar, and observe the drama from a higher perspective to find a solution that works for all parties involved.

If you develop this gift and apply it, your life will become more balanced, enjoyable, and productive. More than that, your spirit guide is inviting you to use this skill to help others. So, incorporate it not only into your day-to-day life but also into your community to create long-lasting positive change.

Authenticity

Many people who work with star beings stand out from their families, friends, and communities. They might have autism, be gay or adopted, have very specific interests, or look different. Sometimes, this can feel like a curse. Especially as teenagers, we don't enjoy being different. Have you noticed this? Have you ever tried to fit in, only to find it didn't work? There was nowhere to hide. However, being different can be a valuable gift that supports you on your spiritual path. Why is that? It forces you to be *yourself*, no matter what. In fact, it's likely that you agreed to tackle this 'problem' in this lifetime and transform it into a healing tool for yourself and others.

Your spirit guide can help you embrace this gift by guiding you into situations that teach you the value of authenticity. Being happy with who you are, even proud of it, can set a great example for others and make our society more inclusive and diverse.

Challenges

Since we live in a dualistic world, everything we do can have positive and negative consequences. While we can always look forward to enjoying the benefits our spirit guides bring us, we also need to be aware of the challenges they may present so we can avoid the pitfalls. With star beings, there are three main risks we need to look out for because they can lead us down the wrong path.

Being ahead of your time

If you're someone who works with a star being, your mind often wanders into the future. You might be planning what to cook for dinner tomorrow, wondering what kind of cars we'll have 100 years from now, or having precognitive dreams. You're always looking ahead. It's part of your purpose here on Earth to be a forerunner and pave the way for others to follow. Your star being guide loves to put you into situations that stimulate this even more.

The challenge you face is that your ideas, values, and way of thinking are ahead of your time. This can rub people up the wrong way if they aren't ready to let go of the past. You might face ridicule, disruption, and frustration. Don't take it personally and don't judge others. Instead, realize this is a sign you're on the right track! The trick is to find people and environments that support your endeavors and let you envision the future for the rest of us.

Struggling to fit in

We've already talked about authenticity, and yes, it's a gift. But it can also be a challenge. One I know well, because I always stood out in small-town Germany, where I grew up. I looked different, had a weird name, was adopted, had parents who spoke with a Dutch accent, and was super-sensitive and a huge introvert. You might well believe that I had trouble fitting in. But nowadays, I know that this challenge was worth taking on. I learnt always to be myself, and my clients love the fact that I'm different and live my life authentically.

Star beings who work with humans also know a thing or two about this struggle. They're universal cultural ambassadors trying to create relationships with us for the benefit of all. So they're experts in intercultural communication and can help us overcome these kinds of difficulties. Remember, working with a specific type of guide always means that we have similar energy patterns to them and so a struggle to fit in is part of the package with a star being.

Finding like-minded people

The third challenge I want to discuss here is that differing from everyone else makes it harder to find like-minded people. Thankfully, we now have technology that makes it easier to find those who share our values and interests. Star being guides have played a major role in this development. Take, for example, the Internet. The famous scientist and inventor Nikola Tesla experimented with the idea of a 'world wireless system' in the early 1900s. He also stated that he'd been contacted by star beings! The Internet was eventually created by scientists who wanted to share their ideas with colleagues. Now we can all use it to find like-minded people across the globe, come together, learn from each other, and share our wisdom. It's made time and space irrelevant.

With a star being guiding you, your personal challenges may be the fuel for other great inventions that will shape the future in big and small ways.

What does your connection to a star being say about you?

Now that you've learnt what star beings are and become familiar with their unique characteristics, gifts, and challenges, let's take a step back and examine what it says about *you* when one of your spirit guides is a star being. What does your connection tell you about yourself?

You have a persistent longing to go home

Have you ever had an intense longing to 'go home'? Even when you were snuggled up on your living-room couch? Working with star beings often invokes this longing, because it means that you've spent at least a few lifetimes on other planets. You might even have spent more time elsewhere in the Universe, which makes things here appear weird, unfamiliar, or downright upsetting. Your decision to incarnate on Mother Earth may be your equivalent of going abroad for a few years. You enjoy the experience, but you get homesick from time to time.

Wherever you have lived before, one reason for your trip to Earth will be to create and express that which you miss most from your previous home. So, is something missing from your life that really triggers you? Is it a feeling, an idea, or something more concrete? Whatever it is, it's your job to introduce the rest of humanity to it in some way, shape, or form. Once you find the right medium to do so, be it art, business, or cooking, you'll be well on your way to living your purpose.

Life on Earth is a mystery to you

You're just a visitor to Earth, so what's normal and acceptable here seems bewildering and irrational to you. You may suffer from social anxiety and not enjoy small talk. The physical limitations of the human body may frustrate you. You're likely to be interested and talented in technology, science, or metaphysics, and able to manipulate energy to heal people or places. You may have distant memories of using telepathy and teleportation. Why aren't those conveniences available now? Other people may consider you strange, weird, or different. Don't let that bother you! All your 'odd' behavior is normal where you're from and your spirit guide understands you because they're from the same place. They know how hard it can be for you to fit in with Earth humans and they're happy to support you in any way possible.

You're a cosmic ambassador

Ambassadors are authorized messengers on a special mission and/ or representatives of their government resident in another country or international organization. You have a very similar role. The difference is that you don't come from another country, but another planet, star system, or even dimension. Instead of a government, you represent the collective spirit of your cosmic home. However, the task is very similar. It's about bringing the soul qualities of your cosmic home to the living spaceship we call Mother Earth and sharing them with all the beings here.

The star being assisting you as a guide is your contact back home, connecting you to the energies you came to channel into this world. You don't have to be a professional channel or medium to do this. You've been channeling energies all your life, right from a tiny baby. Your smile, voice, presence, and personality all express the faraway light that shines in your heart. So all you need to do is to be yourself. That's enough to complete your mission.

You aren't the only cosmic ambassador here. If you let your star being help you, they'll guide you to others, so you can work together and celebrate the diversity of life in all its forms.

Star being communication across cultures

Star beings are found as spirit guides all across the world. Few major religions or spiritual traditions mention them, but many indigenous people speak of their connection to the stars. Some researchers also argue that Hindu gods like Shiva and Vishnu and Egyptian gods like Ra and Osiris originated elsewhere in the Universe. My spirit guides have never spoken to me on that subject, so I can't tell you if it's true, but it's an interesting idea to ponder.

Also, if we agree that the stars themselves are sentient, and therefore star beings, as the name implies, we can find a whole range of traditions based on the relationship between humans and star beings. The ancient Shinto religion comes to mind. It states that the emperors of Japan are descendants of Amaterasu, the sun herself. The equivalent in Greece would be Apollo, the national divinity. The high priestess known as the Pythia, the Oracle of Delphi, was his official channel and messenger. Her visions influenced everyone in the ancient classical world, from foreign emperors to local farmers. All came to seek advice.

In modern times, many small spiritual communities have developed around star being communication. They often base their beliefs on the works of researchers like Erich von Däniken and Zecharia Sitchin, who popularized the idea that aliens visited the planet in ancient times and influenced human history in significant ways. These theories also serve as the foundation for the starseed movement. This is neither an official organization nor does it have a centralized authority, nor a codified belief system. Instead, people use the Internet to connect with one another and share their experience of being a soul that originated elsewhere in the Universe – another planet, star system, galaxy, dimension, or parallel Universe – and is now incarnated as a human to assist in the evolution of life on Earth.

If we look at these examples, we can recognize some common threads when it comes to communicating with star beings. The one that stands out the most is that galactic messengers incarnate as humans, be it as leaders of countries or our next-door neighbors. There are reports of this throughout history, from the olden days, when emperors and kings legitimized their reign with their off-planet ancestry, to today, when thousands of individuals channel the Pleiadians, Sirians, and Andromedans. Chaneling is, along with meditation, a very effective method of connecting with this type of spirit guide. It's the ability to let your spirit guide directly speak through you while you remain in a trance-like state. People attempting to contact a star being can learn both channeling and meditation. I recommend the book *Opening to Channel* by Sanaya Roman and Duane Packer.

Receiving the call

Spirit workers throughout history and across the world who have had a star being as one of their spirit guides have received the call to work with them in the following ways:

- a fascination with one of the spiritual traditions that work with star beings

- an ancestral connection to a specific star being

- repeated synchronicities that involve a star being

- dreams that feature this type of guide

It's up to you to create a unique communication style to use to converse with your star being spirit guide. Review what you learnt in this chapter. Which parts resonated with you on an intuitive level? Which parts didn't make much sense to you? And what would you like to try or learn more about? If you wish, you can make notes in your workbook (*see Bonuses, p.243*), ready for when you get to create your own ritual to connect with the specific star being you're working with.

STAR BEINGS AT A GLANCE

Characteristics: Cosmic consciousness, able to harness energies, an affinity for technology

Gifts: Energy healing, a healthy detachment from human drama, authenticity

Challenges: Being ahead of your time, struggling to fit in, finding like-minded people

What having this type of spirit guide says about you: You have a persistent longing to go home, life on Earth is a mystery to you, you're a cosmic ambassador.

Next, we'll look at angels – their characteristics, gifts, and challenges, and how humans have worked with them throughout history and across cultures.

~

Chapter 10

ANGELS

In the beginning of my spiritual explorations, I always skipped angels, because they only seemed connected to Christianity. Since I'm not religious, I avoided the topic altogether. I also didn't like how they were almost always portrayed as European-ancestered blond, blue-eyed females in white gowns. I couldn't identify with them at all. This changed in 2016, when I discovered Kyle Gray's books about angels.

I'd just realized that my encounters with non-physical beings over the last 15 years of my life had a purpose: I could use my ability to receive information from the spirit world to help people. This prompted me to learn as much as possible about spirit communication of any kind. So I decided to learn more about angels and how to connect with them. I immersed myself in the topic and read anything I could find about these heavenly helpers. I found myself mostly drawn to Kyle's books and this set the stage for what was to happen one sunny afternoon.

I was working on my laptop, as I often do in the afternoons, when I sensed a presence and looked out of the window. What I witnessed was incredible: 40 to 50 angels on the rooftops of the surrounding houses, all looking at me! No one else could have seen them, because they hadn't quite taken on full physical form but were in the dimension that lies between our 3D reality and the dream state. I could see them with my own eyes, but I couldn't have touched them. They weren't wearing white gowns and didn't all have blond hair. In fact, they were dressed in T-shirts, jeans, summer dresses, and other modern clothing items, and looked like everyday people from around the world. If it hadn't been for the wings and the fact that the surrounding air suddenly felt denser, I'd never have known what they were.

As my mind identified them as angels, my heart burst open to receive a wave of love that brought tears to my eyes. At that moment I understood that my perception of angels as a purely Christian phenomenon was wrong. Just like the other types of spirit guide, angels are non-denominational and help people of all religions and spiritual lineages. They're high-vibrational beings who exude pure love. There's no other type of spirit guide that carries that kind of peaceful energy.

Their message for me that day wasn't passed on in words or images, but through their presence. All religions and spiritual traditions, whether they're being followed by millions today or have been long forgotten by history, have the same core message: follow love, not fear. They use different words, imagery, and rituals, according to their own cultural understanding of the world, but their essence is the same. You might dress in black when mourning the death of a loved one, for example, while someone else will dress in white, but both of you are doing it to celebrate the love that connects you with the person who has departed. There's no reason to fight about outer appearances. Focusing on the intention behind the man-made façade is where we find our commonalities and, therefore, peace.

On a logical level, I'd understood this a long time before. However, it's a different thing altogether when you experience it in the core of your being. That's what happened to me that day. That visit by the angels made me realize that we're all one on a deeper level than I'd ever experienced before.

What exactly are angels?

If you were born into a society influenced by an Abrahamic religion (Christianity, Judaism, and Islam), you might assume you know about angels already. Since the impact of these spiritual traditions on the fabric of these cultures is immense, you'll have encountered angels even without a religious upbringing. From Valentine's cards to shop decorations, they're everywhere. This means you'll have preconceived ideas about what they are, what they're about, and what they look like. If you were born into a culture that draws its values and beliefs from other spiritual traditions, you'll be less imprinted by ideas about this type of spirit guide. Either way, it's time to uncover what angels really are and what you can learn from working with them, since all of us have at least one angel in our team of spirit guides.

The word 'angel' comes from the Greek *aggelos*, which means 'messenger.' This makes sense, since angels act as intermediaries between us and the Divine. They've been around for a while – the Sumerians, Egyptians, ancient Greeks, and Romans all described them. Nowadays, polls show that 55 percent of all Americans say that they don't just believe in angels but have been 'protected from harm by a guardian angel' (*What Americans Really Believe*, Baylor University Press, 2008). How incredible is that? It shows that every single one of us has a guardian angel who provides us with love, encouragement, inspiration, and protection. Angels are the peacemakers, comforters, and healers of the Universe. But they can also crack a good joke or dole out tough love if needed. An unexpected fierceness can come out when they need to protect us from harm.

Some people say angels can't incarnate as human beings. Others tell stories of them taking on human form to bring important messages or save them from harm. I haven't formed an opinion about this yet, since I have no evidence for either theory, and I'll leave it to you to make up your own mind. What I do know is that angels often show themselves as human-like to make it easier for us to connect with them. It's not that they're actually male or female, have blond or black hair, or use their wings to fly around the Universe, they just know that it's difficult for us to communicate with a being made of pure light energy, so they try to make it easier for us by projecting an image that we can understand and relate to. Another way they show themselves to us is as streaming white lights or orbs during meditation, when falling asleep, during dreams, or on waking. They also like to leave white feathers for us to find in unexpected places.

The most famous angels are the archangels: Michael, the protector; Raphael, the healer; Gabriel, the nurturer; Zadkiel, the transformer;

Uriel, the light-bringer; and Metatron, the celestial scribe. Yet even these high-ranking angels don't want us to worship them. This doesn't mean we can't pray to them if we feel called to do so, but it's important not to create an imbalanced relationship. They're different from but not better than any other sentient beings in the Universe, including us. They'll offer help, but we need to ask them for it. Only then will they be able to assist us. Otherwise, they would violate our free will, and they can't do that.

Guide characteristics

There are many different angels – archangels, guardian angels, inspirational angels, manifestation angels, business angels, healer angels, and more. They have different purposes and abilities, but they all share certain characteristics that set them apart from the other six types of spirit guide. Let's look at these in more detail now.

High-vibrational

Angels are very high-vibrational beings, since their essence is pure love and light. What does that mean? They don't know fear and therefore can't act on it, as we humans do from time to time. This is because duality, which is based on the fear/love dichotomy and rules our 3D world and physical existence, doesn't constrict them. Therefore, they can exist on an energy frequency that allows them to have pure thoughts and intentions at all times. They can't wish us harm, be resentful, or have selfish motives. None of that makes any sense to them because they understand we're all one and would just hurt ourselves if we inflicted emotional or physical pain on one another. This doesn't mean angels are pushovers and will let us take advantage of them. It does mean our angel guides can inspire us to live a life based on love and instill the courage in us to do so even in the face of fear.

Loving

When my angel guide is around, I feel a wave of love hitting me in the heart chakra. This is because angels are loving creatures and reside on the frequency we perceive with our heart. They can't help but perceive everything through the eyes of love. I'm not talking about romantic or even sexual love – both can only exist in a dualistic world. The love of an angel is unconditional, knows no boundaries, and doesn't distinguish between who's worthy of it and who isn't. They love every being the same, be that a human, a butterfly, or a tiny pebble on a beach that no one else has ever paid attention to. And yes, even rapists, murderers, and other people we don't want around our children or ourselves have an angel with them who loves them unconditionally. This doesn't mean they condone their actions, but they understand that deep down everyone is a divine spark of light and has the right to be loved. Even if they've veered off the right path.

Non-judgmental

Another characteristic all angels have in common is the fact that they view us as the magnificent beings we are. Remember I told you they don't want to be worshipped? That's why! They realize we're just as amazing and incredible as they are, just in a different way.

Therefore they'll never judge us or compare us to others, because they can see into our soul and they admire what they find there. They don't make fun of our large nose, think less of us because we've just lost our job, or abandon us because of a mistake we've made. Angels want us to let go of all the judgments we subject ourselves to. Next time you look in the mirror, try viewing yourself through the eyes of your angel guide and forget about all the flaws you usually perceive. Instead, focus on discovering the hidden gems inside your soul. The more you can see yourself through the eyes of your angel guide, the higher your own vibration and the vibration of your life will become.

Gifts

Angels make powerful spirit guides, since they can bestow beautiful gifts upon us that can transform our lives in many positive ways. In the holy texts of the Abrahamic religions we find many examples, from Archangel Gabriel announcing the birth of Jesus Christ in the Bible to the revealing of the Koran to Muhammad, and from Archangel Michael, according to the Islamic faith, bringing rain to Earth to the Hebrew language being a gift from the angels, according to Judaism. And even though we might not be prophets or scholars, we can still expect to receive the three gifts I'll discuss next.

Healing of emotional issues

By now you know that angels are all about unconditional love and are trying to inspire us to see the world, ourselves, and our fellow humans through that same lens. This allows us to focus not on the flaws, imperfections, and shortcomings of others, but on the beauty of their soul. They therefore feel validated and seen, which allows them to bloom and let their light shine without shame and inhibitions. This is a transformational process that's very healing.

We often require healing, because trauma can leave us stuck in emotions like shame, guilt, and anger. These are a natural reaction to trauma and will pass once we've processed them. However, we often don't process them, but try to suppress them, hide our state from others and ourselves, and lock it all away in our psyche. Then we feel stuck, disconnected, and abandoned by the higher powers. Working with our angel guide can provide the emotional healing we require.

Resolving of fears

Related to emotional healing is another angelic gift: resolving fundamental fears. Love and fear are the spiritual building blocks of our dualistic world. We need both in our human incarnation to gain the wisdom we came here to acquire. Fear warns us when we take the wrong path or are in danger. However, it can also arise as a result of negative experiences in the past that are still dictating our behavior in the present and therefore will lead to undesired results in the future. This kind of fear is unhealthy and blocks us from living a happy and fulfilled life.

Angel guides can help us shift the balance toward love and away from fear. They give us this gift through allowing us to experience the love they feel for us and all living beings. All we have to do is open up to their presence and their guidance, which they send through symbols, synchronicities, and intuition. Then, once we've learnt to connect with our angel guide fully and have conquered our fears, we can assist others through their own process of returning to love.

Compassion for all beings

Compassion is a concern for the sufferings and misfortunes of others. It requires empathy, which is the ability to understand and relate to what other people are experiencing. Some of us are born with this gift and let it permeate everything we do in life. Most of us gain it by living through hard times ourselves. However we've acquired it, our angel guide can enhance it. They'll do so by opening our heart to increase our perceptiveness. This can be scary in the beginning, because now we sense so much more. We take note much more quickly when others feel sad or angry, or are in physical pain. Once we get used to it and understand how not to let it overwhelm us to the point where we take on the emotions as our own, we'll realize this sensitivity is a gift that will serve us well in pursuing our dreams and aspirations. It'll also serve in making this world more inclusive and egalitarian for all.

Challenges

Yes, challenges can come from working with angel guides, and boundary issues often lie at the heart of them. These problems arise if we try to live the life of an angel instead of a human. Some of us over-identify with the angelic realm and therefore lose our footing in the 3D world. If this happens, we also lose the ability to set the boundaries that are essential for life as a human being. Let's discuss the three challenges that can arise from this problem.

Gullibility

Earlier in this chapter, I encouraged you to see yourself, the world, and others through the loving eyes of your angel guide. However, if you ignore your more unpleasant feelings and pretend only to see love and light instead of acknowledging and working through issues and problems as they arise, you weaken your emotional alarm systems. These tell you if you can trust someone or not by making you either feel connected, curious, and loving, or fearful, cautious, and angry. If you often avoid the latter emotions, these warning systems lose their power, just like unexercised muscles do. This means you leave the door wide open for people who only have their own self-interest at heart and will try to take advantage of you.

Realize there's a reason you're a human and not an angel. You incarnated to accomplish your life purpose and it's essential you do it here, on Earth, in the flesh, not in the angelic realm. Remember, your angel guide loves you just the way you are, human flaws and all. They don't want you to try to be them. It serves you better to use their guidance to become the best version of yourself here on Mother Earth.

Ungroundedness

The same root problem can make us ungrounded and cause us to lose touch with reality. The more we try to reach angelic levels and 'fly off' to escape the harshness of everyday life, the more life will restrict us to 'bring us back down.' Life also sets boundaries for us when we fail to do so ourselves. I can tell you from personal experience that money problems are one limitation we can encounter when we don't ground ourselves enough. It's not an unfair punishment. It happens because the Universe is trying to show us we aren't present enough in our life to accomplish what we came here to do. These difficulties catch our attention and ground us here on the Earth plane.

What your angel guide wants you to know is that being grounded doesn't just mean connecting to the Earth via meditation and visualization. It means taking part in life, fulfilling our obligations, and taking practical steps to live with purpose every day.

Becoming too idealistic

The third challenge that can arise from having an angel as a spirit guide is walking around with rose-colored glasses. Again, this happens because of porous boundaries between us and the angelic world. An optimistic outlook on life is great. As is the wish to create more inclusivity and equality. Angels want that too. However, if we become too perfectionist, we set ourselves up for failure. Constantly comparing our vision of an ideal world with our human reality can result in depression, anger, and apathy. It's important to learn to hold a vision and be realistic at the same time. That's how we can make our dreams of a better future come true.

What does your connection to an angel say about you?

So far you've learnt what angels are and become familiar with their unique characteristics, gifts, and challenges. Now, what does it say about *you* when one of your top three spirit guides is an angel, according to the quiz? What does your connection tell you about yourself? From doing thousands of readings as a spirit guide medium, I've learnt there are three things that make you stand out from other people.

You're a highly sensitive soul

The fact that an angel is one of your main guides tells me you're a highly sensitive person. Contrary to what society sometimes wants us to believe, that's a good thing. Yes, even if you're a guy! High sensitivity isn't a sign of weakness, powerlessness, or being a pushover. Yes, you want to work on your boundaries. Otherwise, you can become overwhelmed by all the impressions that reach you from the outside world and the spiritual realms. But if you do your boundary work, you'll be empowered to become a real channel for good and to bring some of that angelic love and wisdom down to our human plane. A river needs boundaries, including a riverbed, otherwise it would never reach the ocean. A drinking straw needs walls to transport the fluid into your mouth. The same is true for you. Without boundaries, your energy will dissipate into nothingness. But when they're strong, your sensitivity can reach new levels without you being overwhelmed and wanting to flee the world because its harshness reaches you unfiltered.

You care for others

Your heart goes out to those in need. Like me, you might not watch the news because of the constant barrage of suffering, sadness, and abuse. It upsets me and makes me either depressed, frustrated, or angry. These moments of vulnerability to the anguish of the world don't feel great. They make you wonder why everyone else seems to be able to just ignore it, don't they? But they also show that you care for others, more so than most other people do. You can't walk past a homeless person, crying child, or neglected animal without deep empathy and compassion welling up. That's why your angel guide wants to work with you. You're both all about service, love, and peace. It doesn't matter how you express those qualities in the world – through your job, volunteering, or just helping wherever you can. The point is giving your caring soul a chance to be of service and fulfill its purpose in one form or another.

You're a healer and bringer of peace

Your sensitive and caring heart isn't just there to make you suffer! Your sensitivity is part of your role as a healer and peace-bringer. Being a healer doesn't mean becoming a doctor or a Reiki master (though you can if you want to); it can happen in all kinds of direct and indirect ways, just like bringing peace. An architect can focus on designing tiny, easily constructible houses for the homeless. A teacher can train their pupils in preventing and resolving conflict. A farmer can create methods of working the land without destroying its natural balance.

Whatever you do, your angel guide is with you to help you bring healing and peace in your own way, without being overwhelmed. When people come and open up to you about their problems, it's a sign you're needed, but it doesn't mean you have to get more involved than you already are. It does mean that you can lend an ear and create the space for them to discover and take the next step of their healing journey or find peace in their lives.

Angel communication across cultures

We mentioned earlier that the Abrahamic religions are all aware of the existence of angels. Some priests, prophets, monks, nuns, and other practitioners of these spiritual traditions have worked with them and left clues about how to connect with them.

A famous example is St Teresa of Avila, a Carmelite nun, mystic, and author who lived during the 16th century. She had many visions of angels that left her ecstatic and at one with God. In the 1930s, another nun, St Faustina, from Poland, prayed to Archangel Michael every day and became famous for seeing angelic spirits in visions and in physical form. There's also Princess Ileana of Romania, who later became the Mother Superior of an Orthodox convent under the name Mother Alexandra. She wrote *The Holy Angels*, a well-researched study of angels from both the Eastern and Western Christian perspectives.

In Islam, belief in angels is one of the six articles of faith. The Prophet Muhammad himself received the Koran from Archangel Jibril (Gabriel) and encountered several significant angels on his journey through the celestial spheres. We also have the famous Persian poet Rumi, from the 13th century, who encountered angels for the first time when he was five years old. This set him on a lifelong spiritual exploration of not just his own faith but also of mysticism as the origin of all religions. A more modern example is Abd al-Hamid Kishk, an Egyptian preacher, author, and activist who lived from 1933 to 1996. Up to 10,000 people attended his sermons each Friday. His book *The World of Angels* is based on the Koran and Hadith, and deals with every aspect of the angelic world from an Islamic perspective.

There are still angel experts today, though they aren't always connected to an organized religion. Diana Cooper, Kyle Gray, and Melanie Beckler have all written books on how to connect with your own personal angel. Kyle mainly uses prayer, meditation, and oracle cards, while Melanie works with channeling, meditation, and also with cards, and Diana prefers oracle cards, meditations, and mantras. A new author on the subject is Claire Stone, who focuses on the female archangels and their re-emergence in our collective consciousness now that the suppression of the divine feminine is lifting. She works with affirmations, invocations, and ritual.

What we can learn from all these angel communicators is that prayer, meditation, contemplation, and channeling are the main means of connecting with angels. It isn't so much about knowing the exact words to a prayer or the right way to meditate, it's more about letting go of the intellect. This way you can drop into your heart space, where you can open up to the angelic realm and connect with angels through feeling instead of thinking.

I mentioned earlier that when my personal guardian angel comes close, I always sense it in my heart chakra. A wave of love makes me drop my mental and emotional shields, I smile from ear to ear, and I remember that we're all one!

Receiving the call

Spirit workers throughout history and across the world who have had an angel as one of their main spirit guides have received the call to work with them in the following ways:

- a fascination with one of the spiritual traditions that work with angels

- sensing an unseen presence that emanates unconditional love

- an ancestral connection to a specific angel

- repeated synchronicities that involve angels

- dreams that feature this type of guide

It's up to you to create a unique communication style to use to converse with your angel spirit guide. Consider what you learnt in this chapter. Which parts resonated with you on an intuitive level? Which parts didn't make much sense to you? And what would you like to try or learn more about? If you wish, make notes in your workbook (*see Bonuses, p.243*), ready for when you get to create your own ritual to connect with the specific angel you're working with.

ANGELS AT A GLANCE

Characteristics: high-vibrational, loving, non-judgmental

Gifts: Healing of emotional issues, resolving of fears, compassion for all beings

Challenges: Being a bit gullible, ungrounded, and too idealistic

What having this type as a main spirit guide says about you: You're a highly sensitive soul who truly cares for others and can't be happy without everyone else being happy too. You're a healer and bringer of peace.

Now that we've finished looking at all seven types of spirit guide, you're about to learn how to connect and communicate with your own spirit team. Are you ready?

～

PART III

HOW TO CONNECT WITH YOUR SPIRIT GUIDES

CHAPTER 11

YES, EVEN YOU CAN TALK TO SPIRIT GUIDES

Since I had no religious or spiritual background, my spirit guides had to convince me they were real and not a figment of my imagination. So, what did they do? They appeared in full physical form to me. No matter how much my mind wanted to use logic to explain their appearance, it was impossible. I asked myself if that very first encounter with my ancestor guide in Germany was a dream. But no, I was awake. My eyes were open. It was no hallucination. I'd taken no drugs and I have no history of mental health issues. I also got independent confirmation only two days after the incident, when I learnt at the Shamanism workshop that spirit guides sometimes transferred energy in the form of glowing red orbs. The encounter was real, there was no doubt about it. I had no choice but to accept the existence of another dimension. Even then, it took me 15 years to put the puzzle pieces together. Only then did I realize what the spirits were trying to tell me and how it would help me teach others how to connect with their own guides.

Encounters with the spirit world can make little sense at first. Sometimes it takes a day or a year, or even a decade to understand their true meaning. That's okay. We might prefer an instant explanation, but the spirit world doesn't work that way. Not expecting spirit guides to play by our rules is part of the mindset shift we need to make if we want to connect with them. If we go into this experience with the wrong expectations, we set ourselves up for failure. Yes, they made it easy for me because they appeared in full physical form, but I still had to adjust my mindset, and no one could do that for me. We all have to do it for ourselves, one new thought at a time.

No worries – I'll help you make that shift. In this chapter I'll explain some core concepts you need to understand before you create a ceremony during which you'll attempt to contact your spirit guides. Even though I can't make your spirit guides physically appear for you, I can help you connect with them in other ways. Nowadays, I don't see many spirits in physical form. I don't need to, because I can connect with them on a telepathic level. It takes a lot of energy for them to manifest in physical form and they prefer not to if it isn't necessary. Seeing them with your mind's eye, or not at all, is just as valid for communication. It's often said that seeing is believing. Here it's the opposite. Some people only hear spirits, or sense them, or even smell them. The form of the contact isn't important. What is essential is the right mindset. You need to stay open to the possibility that spirit guides are real and that you can communicate with them. It's just like any other goal – you need to believe it's possible to reach it, otherwise you'll never make it.

That doesn't mean you have to become gullible or naïve. It means you want to give yourself a fighting chance of experiencing something without preconceived judgments hindering your progress. As someone who grew up convinced that astrologists, psychics, and mediums were all charlatans, I understand that reversing belief systems is a work in progress. That's one reason you can't expect immediate results. It takes patience, perseverance, and regular practice. It takes practice to switch easily from the logical mind we use for everyday tasks like shopping or writing an email, to the more intuitive mind we need to connect with the spirit world. There's no finish line either – it's a lifelong learning experience. Even spirit workers who have done this kind of work for 30 or 40 years learn something new every day.

That said, I want to remind you that everyone can communicate with their spirit guides. Yes, even you! You don't need any special skills and you needn't be a professional spirit worker. Let's look at the four mindset shifts that will help you do it.

Spirit language

The first mindset shift that will help you prepare for your very first spirit guide ceremony is letting go of the assumption that spirit guides communicate the same way humans do. They don't. So, how do they communicate and how does it differ from human language? We're used to getting a message across through the spoken or written word. Spirit guides might use these, but they mostly communicate through symbols, dreams, and intuition.

Symbols

It's important to realize that symbols aren't universal; they mean different things to different people. We often associate a rose with romantic love, for example, and so people assume they need to interpret it that way. This isn't true. If your grandma always smelled like roses, then a rose represents your grandma to you, not romantic love. Always check in with yourself first before interpreting a symbol. What does it mean to you? Does it remind you of someone or something? What emotions does it evoke? What thoughts or events or people do you associate with it?

Symbols aren't always visual. Smells, sounds, and sensations can all be symbols too. The sensation of flying can be a symbol of freedom. The sound of a laughing child can represent a vacation destination we visited when we were a child.

Spirit guides use symbols to communicate in dreams, but also when we're awake. Pay attention to any daydreams and fleeting visions that you experience during the day. We often ignore these because they're so subtle. They don't seem relevant to what we're doing (or so we think). But once we sensitize ourselves to them, we'll notice recurring themes and symbols. The more we bring these into our awareness, the easier it will be to interpret them.

So, stay alert. Your guides can also draw your attention to symbols in the outside world. Number sequences can appear on alarm clocks and number plates. Other symbols can show up in billboard ads, on TV, or in books. Many mediums create a symbol dictionary to learn the symbolic language their spirits use. For me, when an angel shows up during a spirit guide reading and they want to talk about my client's work life, they come wearing a business suit. It's a symbol that helps start the conversation.

These symbols are always personal. Look out for the ones your team use.

Dreams

Another form of symbolic language that your guides use to communicate with you is your dreams. They don't influence all your dreams. You can tell by the intensity. If a dream is very vivid, appears to be almost more real than the waking state, and makes your intuition tingle, then it might be a dream with a message. I can tell the difference by how I wake up. If I've reached a deeper sleep state than usual and I take a long time to regain consciousness, I know I need to pay attention. It's almost as if I've come back from a diving trip and am struggling to reach the surface. I'll also still be tired and could take a nap just to recover from the intensity of the dream.

An example would be a dream I had 20 years ago. In it, a spirit guide disguised as an older lady with long white hair told me it was time. While she said that, she pointed down a little path. Even though she didn't mention it, I knew it led to the south of France. I realized this was a significant dream, but didn't know how to interpret it. Then, in 2017, I was invited on a month-long writers' retreat at a castle in southern France. That's where I started writing the book you're now holding in your hands. The dream had foreshadowed my journey as an author.

Remember, the symbolism in a dream is personal. Form your own interpretation before consulting a book or the Internet. Once you've had the same symbol multiple times, make a note in your spirit guide symbol dictionary.

Intuition

Intuition is a powerful tool that most of us underestimate. Western culture prefers logic and sometimes even ridicules our intuitive senses. However, the more sensitive we allow ourselves to become, the better our intuition functions, and it picks up subtle information that would otherwise get lost. When we develop our intuition, it can turn into psychic and mediumistic abilities and allow us to communicate with the spirit world.

Our spirit guides use our intuition all the time to send us messages, but often in vain because we aren't paying attention. But the more we follow our intuition, the more positive results we'll see, so the more we'll trust it, and the closer our connection with our guides will become. Next time you go for a walk, don't pick a destination beforehand, just follow your intuition and see where it takes you. If you have the choice between two books, pick the one that intuitively feels more interesting to you. Practice making little decisions based on your intuition. That way there won't be any negative consequences to deal with if something goes wrong. Then, once you've built trust, move on to bigger ones. Your guides are always ready to help you, but, as with any other relationship, it takes time to establish good communication.

Spirits or imagination?

Is it my spirit guides or just my imagination?

The second mindset shift I want to help you make is about wondering if you're just making things up. Our guides are communicating with us all the time, but our ego often dismisses their messages as our imagination. We don't even realize how much information gets filtered out and suppressed because of this. Some people even doubt their own sanity. They wonder if they're suffering from schizophrenia or other mental health issues, when in reality they're just receiving messages from their spirit guides. Carmel Joy Baird, a medium from Canada, spent years hiding from the world because she assumed there was something wrong with her. When she discovered that she was 'just' a medium, it was a huge relief and she could transform her life.

A 2015 study from Harvard Medical School found that 5 percent of the general population see and hear things that aren't physically there. Other studies mention 28 percent of any general population. While we stigmatize these phenomena in Western culture, they can be an important part of other people's religious or spiritual beliefs. Many people regard them as a positive part of their lives. Carl Jung, the founder of psychoanalysis, had regular conversations with his 'imaginary' friend Philemon during his adult years.

Some cultures distinguish between people with real problems and people who can talk to spirits. The latter receive training by professional spirit workers to hone their talents and use their gifts to help the community. In Western society, we often assume that hearing voices or seeing things others can't see means we have mental problems. Of course, these experiences can be signs of psychotic disorders such as schizophrenia, bipolar disorder, borderline personality disorder, major depressive disorder, or PTSD. Or other problems, such as Parkinson's disease, narcolepsy, dementia, brain tumors, and epilepsy. So, how do you know that your experiences aren't signs of mental health issues? Well, statistically, these only account for 25 percent of people reporting such phenomena. Symptoms of mental health problems, schizophrenia in particular, start between the ages of 16 and 30. There are gradual changes before obvious symptoms start. Delusions occur, such as believing you're Jesus or a famous actor. You might think you can fly or that the FBI is out to get you. Others will notice confused talk that doesn't seem to make sense, and sometimes movement disorders. You could become catatonic, have a lack of pleasure, trouble with speech or a dull, flat-sounding voice. You could become apathetic, stop bathing or taking care of yourself, and even develop a general lack of interest in daily life. Finally, you could have suicidal thoughts and behavior. If you don't show any of these symptoms, chances are that you're fine. I'm not a medical professional, though, so if you have doubts, please do consult one.

Once craziness is eliminated, you need to distinguish between real spirit guide communication and imagination. However, there's a close connection between imagination and psychic abilities. It's often through the channels of the imagination that psychic and mediumistic ability emerges. So don't dismiss the originality of your mind. A dream, for instance, can be a product of your imagination *and* a message from your guides. Guided visualizations also work with your capacity to fantasize. They use it to get to a deeper level than the imagination.

However, here are some signs that can establish the difference between imagination and communication. If your inner voice starts a sentence with 'I,' for example, it often shows that it originated with you. If it starts with 'you,' it's more likely to be coming from an independent source outside yourself.

Also, thoughts and feelings based on fear, not love, aren't coming from your cosmic helpers, but from your own ego. It's not in your guides' interest to scare you. Yes, they might warn you if you're in danger, but they'll give you a solution, not just spread doom and gloom. They might say: 'Turn left now!' to help you avoid a car crash, but they would never say, 'You'll die in a car crash today.'

The same is true if the communication seems discouraging or belittles you: that's your ego. Remember, a spirit can only be your spirit guide if they're connected to you in unconditional love. They have no interest in mistreating you. Those kinds of inner monologue originate in trauma, internalized fears, or self-esteem issues.

Another sure sign is a communication feeling forced. That won't be coming from your guides either, but from you trying too hard to establish a connection and your ego taking it as an opportunity to make things up.

If you find it's your ego communicating with you, not your guides, that's okay. Just take a deep breath, relax, and try again.

Finally, how can you recognize real messages from your spirit guides? The most obvious way is verifying the message through outside sources like the Internet. But that's not always possible.

Another obvious tell is if you hear or see your guides objectively. This means it happens outside you, not inside your mind. However, often a message comes subjectively, from inside you. You see something with your mind's eye or you get an intuitive download. This is harder to distinguish from your imagination. If this is the case, see if you can change the message, vision, or inner voice. If you can't, it's your guides. Also, if the experience seems very vivid and appears out of nowhere like a sudden insight, it's often a message from your guides.

Another clue is if your guide sends a calling card before starting the communication. A calling card is their way of letting you know that they're around. It could be a wave of love washing over you, the air pressure changing around you, a pleasant smell, music only you can hear, and much more. You could suddenly feel hot or cold. In the end, it all comes down to trusting your intuition and getting lots of practice.

Ready? Equipped with the aforementioned tips, you should find it much easier now to connect with your guides. You got this!

Sitting in the power

The third mindset shift you want to make is around quieting your mind and raising your vibration. This is an essential step to connecting with your guides. Their communications can't get through to you unless you know how to quieten your everyday thoughts and raise your energy to match theirs.

Let's talk about quietening your mind first. I realize you might have tried meditating before and not liked it. Well, this is different.

It's not about shutting off your thoughts. That's not even possible. Quietening your mind means not paying attention to your thoughts. The trick is to see them as independent of you. View them as you would clouds. Let them pass by.

The second part is about raising your vibration. Don't worry, you don't have to go vegan. Or join a monastery. Of course you can if you want to! But you can raise your vibration in the comfort of your own home without living a saintly life. All it takes is some practice. Why do it? Because spirit guides reside in a dimension that has a higher energy level than ours. They have to do a lot of work to come down to our level. To help them out, we raise our energy to meet them halfway.

We can both quieten our mind and raise our vibration through a specific meditation developed by Spiritualists called 'Sitting in the Power.' I learnt it from my mediumship teachers Gordon Smith and Tony Stockwell. They've developed their own versions of it, and over the years I've come up with my own too. It has seven steps and I'll share it with you here.

∼ SITTING IN THE POWER ∼

STEP 1

Find a quiet and safe space where no one will disturb you for the next 20 minutes. Close the door, let your loved ones know you're unavailable, and switch off your phone. Don't lie down. Instead, sit on a chair. Make sure you're comfortable, your back is straight and supported, and your feet are touching the floor. Rest your hands on your lap. Close your eyes.

Step 2

Take three deep breaths in through your nose and out through your mouth. Then let your breath find its own rhythm. Pay attention to how your breath fills your lungs and then leaves your body again. Do this for a count of 30 breaths. If any thoughts pop up and you catch yourself getting distracted by them, that's okay. No reason to get upset. Just bring your focus back to your breath.

Step 3

Now shift your focus to your root chakra at the base of your spine. This is one of the seven energy centers (chakras) in your body. Tune in to it. If you can sense it, great. If you can't, visualize a pulsing red light in that spot. Breathe into this chakra for seven breaths. Now, visualize roots growing out of it. Let them wind their way down to the floor and into the earth. Once they reach the center of the planet, they wrap around a giant crystal. You've now created a connection to Mother Earth that will ground and protect you. Inhale her energy and let it fill you up from top to toe. Do this for 10 breaths.

Step 4

Focus on your crown chakra, which is at the top of your head. If you can't sense this energy center, visualize it as a pulsing purple or white light. Open it by visualizing a little door, window, or eye in that location. Breathe into this chakra for seven breaths. Then visualize a beam of white light going straight up from it and connecting you to the center of the Universe. You're now connected to the infinite wisdom of the cosmos. Inhale its energy into your body and let it fill you up from top to toe. Do this for 10 breaths.

Step 5

Focus on your third chakra, which sits in your solar plexus area. This is your power center. Tune in to it or visualize it as a pulsing yellow light that looks like a sun. Breathe into this chakra for seven breaths. Now visualize this bright yellow sun expanding with each breath. Let it grow until it encompasses your chest and belly, then your entire body. Let it expand even further until it fills up your entire aura and builds a cocoon of light around you. You've now built a sacred space filled with your personal power. Optionally, you can also visualize a layer of protection around your sacred space like a bubble of white light.

Step 6

Sit in your sacred power bubble for another 20 breaths. Pay attention to how your personal power field feels. Expect nothing to happen, but if any physical sensations, emotional feelings, or thoughts arise, take note. Then go back to your breath.

Step 7

Visualize your third chakra sun getting smaller with each breath until it's back to its normal size. Then close your crown chakra by visualizing the door, window, or eye closing again. Take three deep breaths in through your nose and out through your mouth. Then slowly bring your consciousness back into the room. Wiggle your toes and fingers. Stretch or yawn if your body asks for it. Open your eyes.

~

'Sitting in the Power' is something I always do with my students at the beginning of a class, practice session, or ceremony. It helps you get in the right mindset for connecting with your guides. Do it at least once a week and ideally two or three times. (Remember, connecting with your guides takes practice.) To make it easier for you, I have a free recorded version of it for you (*see Bonuses, p.243*).

The six clairs

The final mindset shift that will help you gain the confidence to connect with your spirit guides is about having the know-how to make that happen. When you want to drive a car, you need to know how. The same is true if you want to build a business or write a book. You can either try until you learn (not a good idea with driving), or you can let someone with experience explain how it works. The same is true for connecting with your spirit guides. If you've never done this before, it makes sense to learn the basics first.

One of the most important basics you need to learn is how to receive messages from your guides. You've already learnt they have their own symbolic language and can communicate via telepathy, but how does that work? Let me introduce you to the six clairs.

Clair is French for 'clear.' The clairs are the psychic extensions of our five physical senses, with one extra sense added. They help us communicate with non-physical beings like our spirit guides. We all have the clairs, even though Western society doesn't value a worldview that includes spirit guides, so most of us have never learnt how to use them.

To develop your clairs, you need to allow yourself to become sensitive enough to pick up information that isn't available to your physical senses. Sitting in the power is one way to develop your sensitivity. You also need to understand that the clairs can receive information objectively and subjectively. Objectively means the information comes from the outside world; subjectively means that it comes from inside you – from your mind, emotions, or memories. Both are valid, though most professional spirit workers receive information more often on a subjective level.

What's also important is that most people have one or two main clairs that they rely on more than the others. So don't just focus on seeing or hearing your guides. They might communicate with you through another clair!

Let's inspect the six clairs one by one.

Clairvoyance

Clairvoyance means 'clear seeing' and is the ability to receive intuitive information on a visual level. This can be about an object, person, spirit, location, or physical event. You might have experienced clairvoyance without even realizing it. It's not as dramatic as it's portrayed in Hollywood movies. The visions can be very subtle and they're usually seen with your mind's eye. Sometimes you might even think you're making them up. They can be like a daydream, a movie inside your head, or a memory. You can also experience them with your eyes open and they can last for just a second. Artists, designers, architects, and other 'visual people' are likely to have clairvoyance as their main clair.

Clairsentience

Clairsentience means 'clear feeling.' It's what makes empaths different from other people – they can perceive other people's emotions and sometimes even pain or other physical sensations. That's why it exhausts them to spend time around groups of people. They also often avoid watching the news or violent movies. They feel everything much more intensely than other people and if they don't use their clairsentience on a conscious level, it can cause all kinds of havoc in their lives. For that reason, it might feel like a curse rather than a gift. But once they understand how it works, they can consciously work with it and it can become their superpower. You can use clairsentience to connect with your spirit guides by communicating through feelings. Don't focus on seeing or hearing your guides, but pay attention to feelings and emotions that contain messages for you.

Clairaudience

Clairaudience means 'clear hearing.' You may have heard stories of people who were saved from a car crash by a voice that warned them just in time. Or heard a voice calling your name when you were just about to fall asleep or wake up. Often clairaudience manifests as a voice inside your own head. It might sound like your thoughts, but once you pay close attention, you can learn to tell the difference between your thoughts and the quiet voice at the back of your head that encourages and guides you. If you're a musician, a sound designer, or are sensitive to sound in general, this might be the way you can best communicate with your spirit guides.

Claircognizance

Claircognizance means 'clear knowing.' You might have experienced it as an intuitive download, sudden insight, or flash of knowledge – 'intuition that appears out of nowhere in the mind.' You don't recognize where the information comes from. You don't see, hear, or feel it, you just know it to be true. It's often facts, information, perceptions, ideas, concepts, predictions, and premonitions. People who are claircognizant are often analytical thinkers, writers, problem-solvers, entrepreneurs, the self-employed, bookworms, and information-gatherers.

Clairgustance

Clairgustance means 'clear tasting' and is the ability to taste things on a psychic level. It's similar to remembering what you had for lunch yesterday – you can taste the food without having it in your mouth. If your grandmother loved baking cookies and all of a sudden, without thinking about her, you taste them while out on a walk with your dog, that's clairgustance. It could mean that her spirit has stopped by to say hello. People who communicate with their guides through clairgustance are often chefs, foodies, and restaurant critics. They love cooking or enjoy other hobbies related to taste.

Clairscent

Clairscent means 'clear smelling' and is the ability to receive intuitive information through smell. It's one of the lesser-known clairs, because it isn't common to have it as a main clair. However, if you're someone with a highly developed sense of smell, like a wine taster or a perfume developer, it might be your way of communicating with your spirit guides. Do you keep smelling a certain flower? Or your granddad's pipe? Take note and see what that smell symbolizes to you.

Now you've learnt how spirit guide language differs from human language. You can differentiate spirit messages from your imagination, quieten your mind, and raise your vibration. You also know about the six clairs you can use to communicate with your guides. Are you ready for your very first spirit guide ceremony?

$\sim$

CHAPTER 12

FIRST CONTACT CEREMONY

A yahuasca taught me the importance and potency of ritual and ceremony. I've taken part in about 10 ayahuasca ceremonies over the years. The very first one showed me how much more beneficial it can be to connect with the spirit world in a ceremonial setting.

Let me first explain what ayahuasca is. The word is a Quechua one, meaning 'vine of the soul' (*aya*: soul, *waska*: vine). Some know it as *yagé*, *nateema*, or *pilde*. It's an ancient recipe from the Amazon. Local indigenous shamans use it to connect with their spirit guides, heal patients, and work for the good of the community. They mix the leaves of the *Psychotria viridis* shrub with the stalks of the *Banisteriopsis caapi* vine. Sometimes other plants and ingredients are part of the brew as well. Once it's prepared, it looks like a thick brown tea. Over the last decade, it's become very popular among Western spiritual seekers, who flock to the Amazon to take it in a traditional setting. Unfortunately, this creates problems for local communities. One is that charlatans give themselves the title of shaman to attract paying customers, even though they haven't been through the rigorous training an ayahuasquero needs. This leads to the improper use of ayahuasca and has even resulted in some deaths, which reflects badly on the indigenous communities and their spiritual traditions. The other problem is, again, cultural appropriation.

As I mentioned earlier, I tried ayahuasca because I'd learnt that it was part of my indigenous ancestry. I wanted to connect with my ancestors by following this tradition. But even though I spent weeks researching and educating myself about the process, I made a big mistake. My partner at the time and I had no access to an expert who could help us. Instead, we ordered ayahuasca online and took it at home. Bad idea! Not because we took the endeavor lightly. We prepared carefully, made sure we ordered from a reliable source, followed a strict diet for three weeks, and cleaned the house from top to bottom. Then we prepared the brew and let it cook for the specified number of hours. We put on all-white clothes, set our intentions, and prayed. The mistake was that we underestimated the effect it would have on us. We'd read hundreds of accounts from people who had taken ayahuasca and we knew what to expect in terms of psychedelic experiences. However, we weren't prepared for the healing effects.

This is a mistake many people make. The power of ayahuasca doesn't lie in its psychedelic visions, even though they can be spectacular. The main benefit is the cleansing we receive on a physical, emotional, mental, and spiritual level. This kind of healing isn't always a fun experience. Most people will go through bouts of diarrhea and vomiting while being confronted with their inner demons. Any unfinished business, suppressed trauma, or delusions will have to be dealt with. There's no escape. In our case, my partner was plagued by a guilty conscience and told me he'd cheated on me. Now I can laugh about it and I forgave him a long time ago. Back then, I wasn't just furious and hurt about the fact itself, but also that he'd ruined my opportunity to dedicate the ayahuasca experience to my ancestral healing. In addition, ayahuasca makes you very sensitive, and the intensity of the emotions I had to deal with was overwhelming.

A few months later, I received a private invitation to attend an ayahuasca ceremony conducted by a Colombian shaman who came to Europe once a year, so I gave it a second try. The ceremony took place in a small circus tent set up in nature. An altar was at the center, along with a small fire pit. All around, participants had placed camping mats, blankets, and pillows to keep themselves warm and comfortable throughout the night. The ceremony started at sundown. After everyone had settled in, the shaman delivered a short speech to get us into the right mindset. He talked about the respect we needed to show the plant medicine and told us that the ceremony was about healing ourselves and the world. We then approached him one by one. He handed us each a little bowl of ayahuasca, then blessed it and prayed over it before we drank it and returned to our seat.

In contrast to my first attempt, it was a beautiful experience. The ceremonial setting run by a professional made all the difference. We were told not to talk to one another to circumvent getting caught up in one another's emotional dramas, and that rule alone made me feel safe and gave me the space to explore my experience. We were all supported throughout. Intermittently throughout the night, the shaman sang *icaros*, which are medicine songs that guide the soul on its journey through the spirit world, and two helpers were there to ensure that everyone was okay.

I spent most of the night outside by a second fire. It gave me something to focus on and a natural energy source. That night, my ancestor guides offered me profound healing and revealed the next step on my spiritual path. I also felt as if microscopic elves were cleaning out every single cell in my body, and afterward I walked on clouds for at least a week.

That was my experience, but connecting with your spirit guides needn't involve ayahuasca or other psychedelic substances. In fact, this isn't the right way for most people, and should only be considered after lots of research, proper preparation, and with an experienced facilitator. There are many other ways to contact our spirit guides, but it's still a good idea to do it in a ceremonial setting. What might that be?

What exactly is a spirit guide ceremony?

To define what a spirit guide ceremony is, we first need to determine what a general ceremony is. According to Wikipedia, 'A ceremony is an event of ritual significance, performed on a special occasion.' So, what's a ritual? According to Merriam-Webster, a ritual 'comprises a series of actions involving gestures, words, and objects, performed according to a prescribed order.' To put it even more simply: 'a ritual is the established form of a ceremony.' The ceremony is the event itself and the ritual is the action that takes place during the ceremony. So we can define a spirit guide ceremony as: 'a ceremony during which we establish a connection with a spirit guide through ritual and intention.'

This way of communicating with spirit guides is common all over the world. In fact, it's the number one way to do so. I can guarantee that, wherever you're from, your ancestors have communicated with the spirit world via ceremonies at some point in history. Worldwide, it's in our blood and in our DNA. The guides themselves are also used to connecting with us this way.

That's one reason why a ceremony is more effective than other ways of connecting with spirit guides. There are other reasons. We talked about this a little when I told you about my first ayahuasca ceremony. Here I want to discuss a different aspect. Nowadays, most people trying to connect and communicate with their guides use guided meditations. There are thousands of them on YouTube. I even created one for my students. However, over time, I realized that the success rate with this method is low. That's not because guided meditations don't work. They're great if you know what you're doing and just need some inspiration to point you in the right direction. However, if you don't know the basics of spirit guide communication or have never tried connecting with your spirit team, they often backfire. Here are some reasons why:

- There's no encouragement to set intentions and prepare yourself properly.

- Twenty minutes or so isn't enough time to let your mind calm down and enter the slight trance state needed to see real results.

- There's no integration time included. Right after the meditation you might rush off to do the laundry or pick up the kids and not give yourself time to process the experience.

- Many people see a guided meditation as a fun activity to pass the time and don't take it seriously.

- The creators of the meditations don't bear the specific type of spirit guide in mind.

- There's no space to bring in your own imagination, preferences, and experience.

A spirit guide ceremony has a very different approach. It has a preparation phase for you to gather your tools, come up with an intention, and designate the space. The ceremony itself comprises setting up the sacred space, grounding and protecting yourself, calling in your guides, and waiting for a response from them. Afterward, you ground yourself again in everyday reality, dismantle your sacred space, and integrate the experience by journaling about your experience.

A ceremony like this can take from two hours to three days. This allows enough time to get in the right mindset. In fact, the more time and energy you invest in preparing, and the stronger your intention, the better your results will be. This is another lesson I learnt from the ayahuasca ceremonies I took part in. If I took a few days beforehand to relax, meditate, journal, and eat healthily, my experience was always deeper. If I rushed around the day before, getting things done, it was more difficult to quieten my mind enough to connect with the spirit world.

Another reason spirit guide ceremonies are so effective is because you create a physical space to work in. It incorporates the four elements, the four directions, rocks, crystals, and more. This helps your body get involved through movement and gestures. You'll also use your breath to direct your spirit toward the realm of your guides.

Finally, regular repetition of a ceremony makes it more powerful and effective. Just like any other activity, it becomes easier, more natural, and more effective the more often you do it. So consider your first spirit guide ceremony just the start!

Preparing for the ceremony

Now you can move on and prepare for the actual ceremony itself. A spirit guide ceremony requires careful preparation. That's why you've been taking notes so far. For this first ceremony you'll work with your main type of guide, the one that came in first place when you took the quiz. Review the notes you created on this type of cosmic helper and use them to plan your ceremony. Are there any colors, foods, clothing, offerings, environment, and other details associated with this type of guide that you can use? You can also incorporate items you associate with the Divine in general.

Under the best circumstances, you'd have three full days for a spirit guide ceremony. We all lead busy lives and we can't always drop out for a full three days in a row, but the minimum time you want to invest is three hours. You can reduce this to one hour once you have some experience, but since this is your first time, three hours is a more realistic time frame. If this seems like a long time, remember that connecting with your guides can create big transformations in your life. They can help you take the next step on your spiritual path, develop your spiritual abilities, find your purpose, and make this world a better place. It's worth it.

You also want to allow your mind, body, and soul the time to prepare and focus on the task ahead. Rush nothing. You can use the following framework repeatedly, though over time you'll want to adjust it to your own needs. Learn from experience, follow your intuition, and see if your guides have any suggestions you can follow up on. For now, here are six steps to prepare for your first spirit guide ceremony.

1. Decide on the date

Look at your calendar and pick a day that allows you to dedicate two to three hours to the ceremony. If you can't make it happen right away, don't worry. Use the time to work through the following five steps.

2. Set your intention

After deciding on a date, the next step is to set your intention. You do this to give your ceremony a focus. It also alerts your spirit guides to what it is you need their help with. This might sound simple. In reality it can take some deliberation. Here are three suggestions that will make your intention more effective:

- Keep to one intention only. If you want to develop your intuition, then focus on that. Don't also ask for help with finding your purpose. You can always conduct another ceremony later. What is the number one thing you want guidance on? What do you want to achieve or develop most in your life right now?

- Don't ask for what you don't want. This would just keep the focus and manifesting power on the negative. Ask for what you want instead.

- Ask to do or be something, not to have something. For instance, don't ask to have the money to buy a new house. Instead, ask to find the money to purchase your dream home or, even better, to be a homeowner. This gives the Universe and your guides a chance to assist you in ways you haven't thought of. It doesn't restrict them to how you think things should unfold.

- For your very first spirit guide ceremony, keep it simple and make your intention to connect with your main type of spirit guide.

3. Collect your objects

Find four objects representing the four elements (water, air, fire, earth) and/or four directions (north, east, south, west). Examples are a bowl of water, a candle, a feather, and a crystal, or stones painted in the colors that you associate with the four cardinal points. Remember to consult your notes and see how you can personalize these for the type of spirit guide you want to work with during this ceremony. If appropriate, clean the objects with water and then charge them by leaving them out in moonlight, or sunlight.

4. Choose your clothes

Decide on the clothes you want to wear. If a specific spiritual tradition intrigues you, don't just imitate it. To make up an example, find out why followers of that tradition wear yellow during their ceremonies. If it symbolizes strength to them, replace it with something that symbolizes the same to you or your culture. Make sure the clothes are clean.

5. Select your space

Designate a sacred space to hold the ritual in. It could be inside or outside. What's important is that it's quiet and safe, and no one will disturb you. Clean the space physically and/or energetically. If you're outside, collect any trash lying around. If you're inside, use organic cleaning products. You could also use local smudging herbs or incense to complete the cleansing. Then say a prayer, notify any local spirits of your plans, and ask them for their blessing and support. If you feel any negativity during this process, find a new spot.

6. Create your altar

Create an altar in the middle of your sacred space. It doesn't have to be fancy. It can be a chair, a windowsill, or a rock. Place on it the objects you've gathered that represent the type of guide you wish to connect with. Consult your workbook if you need some inspiration on themes, colors, and items. Also add a pen and paper. You'll use these when you close the ceremony.

Conducting the ceremony

The time has come! Now you've prepared everything, you're ready to embark on your very first spirit guide ceremony. Here we'll look at what to do during the ceremony. But first I want to reiterate a few important points:

- Don't worry about making things up. Your imagination is your friend and even if you're using it, your guides will still be able to sneak in a message for you. So, let go. Stop worrying. The more you can do that, the better your experience will be.

- All information coming through is relevant. It doesn't matter if you think you've made something up, if you think your ego is playing tricks on you, or if your dog interrupts you by sitting on your lap. It's all part of the experience and the message.

- Trust yourself, your intuition, and your guides. Don't overthink things. Don't second-guess yourself.

- Send your inner perfectionist on vacation. You can't get this wrong. Even if you think the ceremony hasn't worked, don't worry. There's something to learn from every experience. Try again another time. Practice makes perfect.

• If you feel dizzy or hot, or freezing, or you tremble, don't panic! This is normal. Your body is adjusting to the high vibrations the ceremony is creating. You'll learn to enjoy these sensations as part of your interactions with your guides.

Now, before you do the actual ceremony, read the following steps to make sure you have everything ready and haven't missed or forgotten anything. Next, turn off all your devices. You don't want to be disturbed or distracted in the middle of the ceremony. Take a shower or a bath and put on your clean ceremonial clothes.

Great, let's go!

SPIRIT GUIDE CEREMONY

• Enter your sacred space. Place the objects that represent the four directions and/or elements one in each of the four directions. Use a compass, perhaps the one on your phone, to determine where they are. If you're using elements, let your intuition determine in which direction to place them. Make sure that there's enough room for you and your altar to fit comfortably in the center of your space. If possible, make it big enough for you to lie down with your arms and legs stretched out.

- Optionally, use salt, crystals, or rocks to connect your objects, creating a circle. If you have enough space, make the circle big enough to dance in.

- Face the altar and state your intention out loud. Vocalizing the purpose of this spirit guide ceremony brings it from the mental state into the physical plane through sound and vibration. Tell your guides you're ready to connect with them. Let them know you want to work with them to do your part in making this world a better place. Assure them you're open to their guidance and then thank them for working with you.

- Now, sit down and get comfortable, but don't lie down. It's fine to use a chair. Nothing is more distracting than a leg that falls asleep.

- Quieten your mind by using the *Sitting in the Power* meditation.

- Call on your spirit guide to step forward into the sacred space you've created. Again, do it out loud. Don't skip this step. Your guides can't help you if you don't invite them to, because you have free will.

- Thank them for coming. It doesn't matter if you don't have proof that they're there. That doesn't mean they aren't.

- State your intention to connect with your main spirit guide out loud again.

- Wait for a reply.

Let me pause here. I know this is the part you've been waiting for, which is why there's so much pressure attached to this step. To circumvent any disappointment, I want to explain how this works and what to expect. The most important thing is to keep your expectations in check. Focus on your breathing, not on getting messages. Your mind needs to be quiet and open. By focusing on your breathing, you're giving it a task, and that leaves room for your spirit guide to step in. If you feel moved to dance or sing or stretch, go for it. If you'd rather quietly sit and meditate, that's fine too.

Just keep breathing and pay attention to any signs that might be coming from your guides. Trust that anything that comes through is a sign. Remember the six clairs and that your main clair might not be clairvoyance or clairaudience. Maybe you're getting really hot or cold, or your nose is itching. The surrounding air might seem denser or more electric than usual. Your body could start swaying back and forth. You could feel you're bigger or smaller than usual. These can be very subtle changes. Whatever is changing for you, take note, and then ask your guide to step out of your sacred space. Is the sensation still there or not? Now ask your guide to step back inside your sacred space. If the sensation disappears when they leave and returns when you invite them back in, it could be your spirit guide's calling card. Repeat the process and see if it happens again. If it does, congratulations! You've had your very first communication with your guide.

Now I know it may have been a very simple sensation and it's unlikely to have answered all your questions, but know that you've communicated with an intelligent being! Next time, you might follow up by asking them a 'yes' or 'no' question. Have them step out of the space (and stop the calling card) for 'no' and stay in the space (so you can keep sensing the calling card) for 'yes.'

Again, this takes practice. So if you can't identify a calling card this time around, don't fret or get angry with yourself. It's okay. There's nothing wrong with you. Try again next time. For now, trust that your guide is present. Enjoy knowing that. Give it at least 15 minutes.

- Once it's time to finish the ceremony, thank your guide for coming. Then ask them to leave your sacred space.

- Take three deep breaths. Wiggle your toes and fingers. Stretch, yawn. Do anything your body asks you to do. Slowly bring your awareness back into the room.

- Grab your pen and paper and write down everything you experienced during the main part of the spirit guide ceremony. Leave nothing out, even if it seems insignificant. If an ambulance passed by and caught your attention, write it down. If the hair on the back of your neck stood up, write it down. It might not seem important to you now, but sometimes later, when re-reading our notes, we realize that we missed signs from our guides. Also, documenting everything helps us to counteract our ego, which might try to rationalize our experience. If we have it in writing, we can't change the story. If you prefer, you can record it as audio or video.

$\sim$

Closing the ceremony

Ending a spirit guide ceremony is just as important as preparing for and conducting it. So, even if, for whatever reason, your ceremony didn't go as you expected, don't leave out this part, otherwise you'll leave yourself open and vulnerable on an energetic level, which might cause inexplicable tiredness, energy loss, and over-sensitivity. Unprocessed emotions may cause you to be irritable and depressed.

∽ CLOSING THE CEREMONY ∾

- Get up and stomp your feet. Then turn toward your altar and clap your hands three times. Both actions help you ground yourself in everyday reality.

- Thank your guide again for working with you.

- Check in with yourself. Are you back in ordinary reality? Any uncommon bodily sensations should have stopped, your vision should be normal, your breathing back to its usual rhythm, and your emotions under control. If not, jump up and down a few times, shake your legs and arms, and put a bit of salt on your tongue or eat some bread. You can also massage your scalp, arms, and legs.

- Leave your sacred space and take off your ceremonial clothes.

- Dismantle the circle and altar. Take all natural materials back to nature, rather than throwing them in the trash. The other objects go back to their place in your home or where you sourced them. While you do this, you can ask your guides and the Universe to use any excess spiritual energy that you've created to go to someone who needs it.

- Cleanse the space energetically. You can use sage, palo santo or copal. I prefer to find something that grows locally, like rosemary, white sage, or mugwort. This helps the environment and honors the local nature spirits. It's very important to clean the space this way, because you don't want energies to linger. If you're outside, you don't know who will use the space later, and if you're inside your own home, you don't want your family members to be exposed to spiritual energies that they might not want to or be able to handle.

- Next, you can go for a walk or do yoga. Or engage in a creative activity like writing, painting, cooking, or gardening. You don't want to watch TV, read a book, or consume other media. Take time for yourself for at least 30 minutes before interacting with others. Even though you might want to call a loved one and tell them about your experience, it's best to let things settle before exposing yourself to the outside world. Whatever you do, don't drive or operate heavy machinery right after the ceremony.

- Over the next few days, stay alert for spirit messages. Often, you won't get a reply during the ceremony, but you will after. Remember, spirit guides communicate through intuition, symbols, and dreams. Keeping a dream journal by your bed (or your phone to record audio or video) is a great idea after a spirit guide ceremony. Take a few minutes every morning to write down what happened while you were asleep. During the day, note any symbols that keep appearing. The most important thing is to follow your intuition. Your guides will help you find the places, people, and situations that can help you move forward on your spiritual path and fulfill your purpose. Stay open and positive, and trust your guides to provide the answers you need. Expect to be guided, but have no expectations about how it'll happen.

∾

Congratulations, you've just concluded your very first spirit guide ceremony! You've opened the door to the spirit world and contacted your spirit guide. They now know you're ready to take on your role as lightworker. This won't go unnoticed and will be very much appreciated.

Now, what's next? Where do you go from here? In the next chapter we'll look at how you can use your connection with your guides to further your spiritual development, manifest your dreams, live your purpose, and make this world a better place.

∼

CHAPTER 13

WHAT YOU CAME HERE TO DO

Now that you've connected with at least one of your spirit guides, I want to remind you that you're a lightworker and here on this Earth for a reason. You're also a spirit worker with a mission. This mission includes creating a happy life for yourself and serving your family, community, and the world at large through your talents and gifts. Don't worry if you don't know how yet. Your spirit team is there to help you every step of the way. There's also no need to know exactly where you're headed in life. Have faith, take one small step at a time, and enjoy the journey.

Living life as a lightworker

Living life as a lightworker is less complicated than it sounds. You don't have to be perfect. You don't have to retire to a monastery and spend the rest of your life meditating. We're all human and most of us live busy modern lives. Align with your own spirit and everything else will follow, including connecting with your spirit guides and the Universe at large.

How do you align with your spirit? Here are five tips that have worked for me. Don't feel pressured to do them all. See which make you feel lighter and more joyful. Lightness and joy are great signs that you're on the right path.

Meditate

The first way to align with your spirit is to meditate. We've already discussed 'Sitting in the Power.' The great thing about doing this meditation on a regular basis is that it exposes you to your very own energy. Most people have never experienced this. Mostly, we focus on the outside world. If we ever do take the time to concentrate on our inner lives, we use it to criticize ourselves, often to the point where we become depressed. 'Sitting in the Power' changes this. While we meditate in this way, we allow ourselves to experience our inner beauty, strength, and spirit. It allows our unique talents and gifts to reveal themselves to us. We thus have the confidence to go out into the world and do our part. We know our worth and aren't afraid to shine our light.

How often should you sit in the power? As often as you can. Once a week for 15 minutes is great. Three times a week or even daily is also great. But there's no pressure. Do what's right for you and what you can fit into your daily life. Just do it regularly and stick to your chosen schedule.

Pray

Another great way to improve your connection with your spirit is through prayer. I'm still working on this myself. Just a few years ago, I associated prayer with religion and so I wasn't interested. Now I've changed my mind. Prayer isn't about reciting words we don't understand from a holy text that originated hundreds or even thousands of years ago. It isn't about begging or submitting to a higher force.

Two simple mindset shifts started me down the path of prayer. One was when I started to understand that prayer was talking to the Universe and meditating was listening for the answer. That made sense to me. The second was when I learnt to use prayer to thank the Universe for what I wanted in advance, instead of perpetuating a lack by asking for it. This aligns us with the law of manifestation by showing we trust that things will work out for us.

Live thoughtfully

My third suggestion is thoughtful living. That sounds very vague, so let me explain. Thoughtful living means making deliberate choices in your life. Don't follow the herd and do what everyone else is doing or telling you to do. Make conscious choices. What do you want to create? What legacy do you want to leave? How do you envision your daily life? These are questions you want to contemplate. As a lightworker with a bigger purpose, it's paramount that you do. You're a unique soul. If you don't do what you came here to do, no one else will, because no one else can.

Serve

The last part of living life as a lightworker is about serving. This starts by serving yourself. That sounds selfish, but it isn't. If you're unhappy, there's no way you can create happiness for anyone else. Meditation, prayer, and thoughtful living are all part of serving and nourishing your spirit and therefore strengthening your connection with your guides and the Universe. Only then are you ready to serve others by finding and living your purpose. We'll talk about that in more detail later in this chapter. Now I want to mention that living your purpose isn't the same as finding the perfect job. It's more about living *with* purpose every day and finding little ways to serve. No matter how you make a living, this is also the best way to discover your purpose.

Also, serving doesn't mean you have to become a healer or a shaman. You can serve as a dad, a diving instructor, a lawyer, or a friendly neighbor.

Know your mission

In the end, living life as a lightworker is about being aware that you're on a mission. You're here to make this world a better place. Your guides will help you do so. Along the way, they'll help you develop psychically, manifest your dream life, and live your purpose.

Psychic development

Before I explain how your guides can help your psychic development, let me define the term. When I talk about psychic development, I mean growing your intuitive, psychic, and mediumistic abilities. You might think these are three separate abilities. They're not. They all lie on the same spectrum, are interwoven, and build upon one another. The six clairs are the tools we use to receive intuitive, psychic, and mediumistic information. How advanced we are in using them consciously determines what term we use to describe the experience. We talk about 'intuition' when we use the six clairs to receive information from our higher self. When we become more sensitive and can receive information about other people, places, and events here in the 3D world, we call it 'psychic ability.' If we allow ourselves to become even more sensitive and pick up information from other realms, like the spirit world, we call it 'mediumistic ability.' I know I've mentioned this before, but it's important to remind yourself that we all have these abilities and can develop them further. Even you. No exceptions!

The benefits of developing our psychic abilities are manifold. The better our intuition becomes, the more our self-confidence grows, because we know we can trust and rely on our higher self. We understand that it'll always support us because it's part of us. Nothing can and will stand between us and our higher self. This knowledge will make us feel less lost and confused in life. We can move forward with certainty and clarity.

Psychic development also improves our relationships with other people, animals, and the natural environment, including plants and trees. This happens because we can sense both them and their needs better. Our compassion grows and we're less inclined to think of our own benefit only. This leads to less loneliness and can prevent depression and feeling disconnected. We realize we're never alone and always surrounded by love.

The last benefit is that communication with our cosmic helpers gets better and easier because we trust our mediumistic abilities more. We understand the underlying principles of the process and don't doubt that we can do it. We've developed our sensitivity enough to pick up on even the subtlest information coming in from our guides. We don't have to put so much effort into connecting with them. We can tune in within minutes and needn't conduct a whole ceremony for each little question anymore.

How can your guides help you with your psychic development? First, you need to ask them to assist you in developing your clairs. They can't assist you if you don't ask. Create a ceremony for this purpose. Decide which of your three top spirit guides from the quiz can help you best in this endeavor. Look over your notes and re-read the chapters that describe those guides. Follow your intuition and make a choice.

Then, using prayers, props, and intentions that represent psychic development to you, start preparing the ceremony. For example, maybe you have precognitive dreams that show you what will happen in the future and you want to develop this ability or understand it better. Get a pillow and a moonstone crystal and do the ceremony in your favorite pajamas. You could even sleep in the spot you've chosen for the ceremony. If you want to work on trusting your intuition more, get some tarot cards and use them to create the boundaries of your ceremonial space. Since we associate intuition with our third eye and the color indigo, find a shirt or a scarf or even nail polish in that color and paint an eye in the middle of your forehead. Get creative and let your imagination guide you. What else do you associate with the kind of psychic development you're seeking? Be innovative and make the ceremony as personalized as possible. The more your energy flows into it, the more successful it'll be.

Once the ceremony is over, you'll find yourself in situations where you can practice using your psychic abilities. Maybe you have to make a small decision, like which book to read next. Use it as an opportunity to practice letting your intuition guide you. Your cosmic helpers will alert you to these occasions and encourage you along the way. Make it a daily game you play with them. You can incorporate using your intuition into your work life and your free time. If you work with people, guess what color their sweater will be that day or what mood they will be in. Are you on the phone a lot? Try to sense if you'll speak to a man or a woman next and what age they are before you pick up. If you do this regularly, you'll see how easy it is to improve your skills. It's fun, too, and gives you a chance to spend time with your guides and get to know them better. You don't have to tell anyone about it if you don't want to. Or you can involve your family, colleagues, and friends if you prefer. Kids love to play these kinds of games and it'll benefit them when they grow up.

Manifesting your dreams

Your spirit guides can also help you manifest your dreams. This is one of the main reasons why people seek to connect with their cosmic helpers. But isn't it selfish to pursue your dreams? I'm here to tell you it isn't. The ability to pay the bills, have a job you love, be healthy, and provide your family with what they need to flourish will enable you to focus on the wellbeing of others. If you're struggling to meet your basic needs, there's no time and energy left to make this world a better place for others. Manifesting your dreams also inspires others and shows them it's okay to want to be happy and fulfilled.

Does that mean your guides will help you become rich and famous? It depends. If being rich and famous will help you fulfill your purpose in this lifetime, then it'll be part of your path. Therefore, your guides can help you achieve it. If, however, your wish is self-serving, it won't happen. Your guides aren't there to serve your ego, but your soul. Your dreams have to be in alignment with what you incarnated to accomplish in this lifetime before your guides will help you manifest them. However, whatever your destiny may be, know that it isn't to live in poverty and misery. We all deserve to feel happy and fulfilled.

My own guides have made it very clear, however, that we can't just rely on our spirit guides to make things happen while we sit at home meditating. We live in a physical 3D world and we need to interact with it and take action daily to create the change we want to see. If we want to be healthy, we need to eat healthily, move our body, and maintain healthy thoughts. If we want to make more money, we need to learn the skills needed to find a better-paid job or start our own business. Manifesting isn't about waiting for a miracle to happen, like winning the lottery. It's about taking small daily steps in the direction we want to go. This shows the Universe we're serious and willing to invest time and energy to make our dreams reality. Only then will it respond by meeting us halfway. So, we need to plan.

Define your goal

First, we need to take our dreams and break them down into goals that we can reach. Without a clear goal, we don't know which direction we should head in and when we've got there. 'I want a better job,' for instance, might sound like a great goal, but it isn't. It's not specific enough. What does 'a better job' mean to you? One that makes you more money? Or one that lets you work from home? Or one that suits your skills better? What do you want to achieve? The more specific, measurable, actionable, results-based and time-bound (SMART) your goal is, the easier it'll be to set up a plan to reach it. 'I want to find a job by January that allows me to be with the kids when they come home from school, makes me x amount of money, and uses my skills as an executive assistant' is a goal that you can take action on. You might not know what that job is yet, but you've set parameters that give as much clarity as possible. Now it'll be much easier to make a list of all the action steps you can take to reach your goal. Then you can move toward it daily. And instead of complaining to family, friends, and colleagues about your old job, you can tell them about your plans and they can give you tips, motivate you, and help you along the way.

Ask for help

Now that you've done your part, it's time to ask your guides for help. You can ask them to assist you with your overall goal or just the next part of the plan to achieve it. Create a ritual specifically for this purpose, using prayers, props, and intentions that represent manifesting skills to you. In astrology, Capricorn is a sign with great manifesting skills. You could draw its symbol on a piece of paper and put it on your altar. Or get a crystal connected to manifestation. Maybe you can use earth from your garden instead of salt or stones to create your circle. Be creative and have fun planning the ceremony. Which guide do you want to work with? Gather crystals, music, flowers, and foods that represent them. Also collect items that represent your goal. If you want to convert your spare room into a home office, for example, you could do the ceremony there, wearing the comfy yoga pants you plan to work in. Or you could create a vision board with pictures of your kids to remind you how happy they'll be to spend more time with you once you find your new job. Create the job ad you'd like to find and place it on your altar.

Once you take steps toward manifesting your dreams, you automatically also start living your purpose, because our dreams are often signs that lead us to what we came here to do. Living your purpose is what we'll talk about next.

Living your purpose

We live in transformational times. Now is the moment for lightworkers to step up and take action. The invention of the Internet is a sign of the times: the beginning of the Age of Aquarius. It's contributed to a lot of changes around the world that impact millions of people on different levels. It's disrupted many traditional industries like news, music, and publishing, as well as how we shop, how we communicate with each other, and more. We're also going through major changes in government, politics, and finance. As always, before new ways of doing things emerge, we go through a phase when everything seems to fall apart. The old ways don't work anymore, which results in confusion and fear for many. This is where lightworkers come in. We trained for this and incarnated at this point in history to help others through these shifts and create a better future for all. We're essential in this transformation process.

If we hide from our responsibility, we'll all suffer the consequences. So, are you ready? Only you can do the job you came here to do. No one else can do it for you, because there's only one you. Either you need to find your purpose or, if you're living it already, go deeper into it. The good news is that you're not alone. Your guides are there to help. They've been sending you signs about this all along. Now it's time to understand and act on them.

However, don't expect your guides to give you super-specific instructions on how to fulfill your purpose. That's not how it works. Our purpose is always a work in progress. It needs modifying from time to time. So our guides give us hints and nudges. If we don't act on them, they'll repeat the message in a million different ways until we get it. This is where many of us get stuck. We want to see the end goal. In reality, living our purpose is more like hiking up a mountain whose peak is shrouded in clouds. Unless we're patient and put one foot in front of the other, we'll never see what the top looks like.

It's all about taking daily action according to the guidance of our cosmic helpers. One day we'll realize that we can look down from that mountaintop and see the path we took to get there and what our life's overall purpose was. It could be as specific as 'developing ways to sell products on the Internet by using feminist principles in the sales process' or as broad as 'making people smile more to raise the general vibration on the planet.' But for now, it doesn't matter where we are in the process of uncovering it, there's always one step we can take in the right direction, even if all we know, for example, is that we want to 'do something with animals.' We don't need to land a dream job in that sector to create change; we could start by volunteering at a local animal shelter or offering to walk our neighbor's dog.

Again, you don't have to know the end goal; all you have to do is live with purpose every day. Then your life's purpose will reveal itself automatically.

As a first step, create a ceremony specifically for this purpose. Ask your guides to reveal one tiny step in the right direction that you can take today. Don't forget to ask them to make it specific, measurable, actionable, results-based, and time-bound. Gather crystals, music, flowers, foods, and more that represent the guide you want to work with and your purpose. You might already realize you like to inspire people, for example. But in what form? Get some magazines and make a vision board that you can put on or hang above your altar. Cut out pictures of motivational quotes and the kind of people you'd like to work with. Wear clothes that make you feel inspired and social. Research what crystals facilitate communication or open the heart chakra. Get creative and have fun with it! Once you get to the part where you open up to a reply from your cosmic helpers, the answer might come in the form of an idea or thought you've had before. Your guides' answers aren't always new and novel. Maybe you've been thinking about welcoming your new neighbors with flowers, but haven't done it yet. Do it now! One of them might be a motivational speaker who is looking for an assistant. You can never anticipate where you'll find the next opportunity to live your purpose!

Once you take steps toward fulfilling your purpose, you also start making this world a better place, because you act as a bridge between the spirit world and our Earthly world. That's what we'll talk about next.

Spiritual activism

You incarnated in this lifetime to make this world a better place. We need less divisiveness, abuse, and fear. All this has the potential not just to destroy humanity, but also many of the other species that live on this planet, not to mention the environment itself. Our self-destructive behavior also affects the other dimensions and realms, since we're all interconnected in ways we can't even comprehend yet. Changing this for the better is a task all lightworkers agreed to take on before they were born. Each of us does it in our own way, using our unique skills, talents, and gifts. I call this work 'spiritual activism.' It's the act of taking spiritual principles and applying them in the physical world. We do so to create a more inclusive, collaborative, and peaceful place for ourselves, our family, our community, and the world at large.

Since you're a lightworker who is also a spirit worker, your spiritual activism takes the form of being a bridge between the spirit world and the human world. You're like a straw through which Spirit flows from one to the other. You're essentially a medium. Not in the traditional sense of delivering messages from spirits (unless you want to), but in the sense that energies that flow from the spirit world can manifest in the physical world through you. This may happen through your creative endeavors as a painter, writer, gardener, or cook. Or through your work with children, animals, or the environment. Or through your life as a stay-at-home dad, an accountant, a student, or an early retiree. The important point is that you're making this world a better place through your actions inspired by Spirit. To be effective in this task, you want to let Spirit move you to take action every day. Even if it's just one tiny thing like answering someone's question on the Internet. Or perhaps one big thing like setting up a non-profit to keep your favorite forest clean. As long as you're acting on spiritual principles like love, compassion, and kindness, you're functioning as a bridge between the worlds and therefore as a spiritual activist.

The most important part of being a spiritual activist is getting your ego out of the way. You don't want to get rid of it, since you need it to survive in our physical world, but you want to move it aside so Spirit can work through you. Earlier, I used the image of a bridge or a straw to explain the work of spiritual activists. Neither is able to fulfill its intended function if it's blocked. That's what happens if you give your ego free rein: it creates fear, and you feel stuck. 'Sitting in the Power' is the best way to practice moving your ego out of the way. It won't disappear, but you can shift it whenever necessary and make it work for you instead of against you.

Each topic we've covered in this chapter is part of becoming a spiritual activist. Spiritual development is essential, because it enables us to communicate with our spirit team. Once we learn how to manifest our dreams, we'll have confidence in our power to change reality and create the change we want to see. And when we discover and live our purpose, it'll give us the method and tools to carry out our spiritual activism. Each skill builds on the others. That doesn't mean that you have to work through them in that order. This isn't a linear path, it's circular. For instance, you might discover a new spirit guide who unveils a new layer of how you can live your purpose. Change is the only constant in life. Start with the area you feel drawn to most at the moment.

To take your first steps as a spiritual activist, ask your spirit guides for help. Let them initiate you as a spiritual activist. What does that mean? It means that you set the intention to help make this world a better place. Then you let your spirit guides know about this intention. Create a ceremony specifically for this purpose, using prayers, props, and intentions that represent a better world to you. Choose one of your main guides to work with. Look at your notes, or the relevant chapter, and customize the ceremony to their characteristics, gifts, and challenges. Now choose an appropriate place for the ceremony and gather the tools, props, music, clothes, offerings, etc., that you'll need. What changes do you want to see in the world? What items represent those changes? If you want to help more women enter the professional weight-lifting world, bring a photo of the current female world champion. If you want more green spaces in your neighborhood, create a ceremony circle with your houseplants. Use your imagination. Anything that puts you into the right mindset will help. Make the ceremony as specific to your intention as possible. Remember, you're a bridge between worlds. Change can happen.

~

MAGIC AND
MIRACLES

Life isn't linear. It unfolds in a spiral and always brings us back to the beginning to start all over again on a higher, more conscious level. At the start of this book, I told you how I discovered that I was living a life guided by Spirit. And that you were too. Maybe you didn't believe me then, even though you felt a calling deep down in your heart, just like I did. You might not have known what it meant or what to do about it, but that calling made you pick up this book. It was Spirit.

I hope that now, after discovering what types of spirit guide work with you and connecting with them through conducting a spirit guide ceremony, you trust and follow that voice that lives in your heart and realize that you do live a life guided by Spirit. You now know of your connection with your cosmic helpers, Spirit's ambassadors, and you possess the tools to communicate with them. Your guides appreciate the time and effort you've put into following the path I've laid out for you in these pages. It makes it easier for them to help you do what you came here to do.

This marks the end of this book and a new beginning for you. You've reached a new level in your spiritual development and are ready for your next step in making the world a better place.

For me, it's time to say goodbye. We've come to the end of our journey together. However, come and find me on social media, say hello, and share your stories with me. I can't wait to hear them. Until then, I'll leave you in the capable hands of your guides. They'll take you through this next phase of your life. If you get confused along the way, lost, or even scared, go back and listen to the voice of Spirit deep down in your heart. If you follow it, you can't go wrong.

In fact, magic and miracles await once you stop trying to do everything on your own and ask your spirit guides to support you on your journey through life. They can help heal trauma from the past so you can look forward, spread your wings, and fly. I hope I've been able to illustrate that through the stories I've shared with you from my life. I went from being an abandoned baby who felt lost and alone all the way into adulthood to healing my emotional wounds, discovering my spiritual abilities, using them to live my purpose, and having the privilege of sharing everything I'd learnt along the way with you.

Your guides will assist you in aligning with your higher self, increasing your trust in the Universe and yourself, developing your gifts and talents, and finding your life's purpose. They'll help you develop the courage and leadership to create the world you want to see – a world that's more inclusive, peaceful, and collaborative. We need you and your vision for the future. Especially if you've been marginalized in the past. We need to include new perspectives to find solutions to the problems we face today.

We can't solve a puzzle if some pieces are missing. And we can't afford to view the world in only one way. Bringing in types of spirit guide that have been ignored in the past is one way of expanding that view. What new perspectives are you going to bring to the table with the help of your spirit guides…?

~

BONUSES

I'm really pleased to make the following materials available at my site. Just visit: **TheSevenTypesOfSpiritGuide.com/bonuses**

1. Workbook

A downloadable workbook, which contains journaling prompts and serves as a place to reflect on what you read, take notes, and gather all the necessary information for your spirit guide ceremony in Chapter 12.

2. Guided Meditation

A guided audio version of the *Sitting in the Power* meditation in Chapter 11.

3. Quiz

The online version of the Spirit Guide Quiz in Chapter 3.

I hope you find these resources helpful on your journey.

ᴀCKNOWLEDGMENTS

I want to thank everyone who supported and encouraged me to become the person I am today. You sat with me during difficult times, listened to my fears and concerns, and let me cry on your shoulder. And you laughed and dreamed with me, and allowed me to see myself in the mirror of your eyes. Or maybe you don't even know me, but your work, your books, and your ideas have inspired me to discover new gifts, talents, and skills inside myself.

I also thank those who challenged me throughout the years, made me face my own fears and shortcomings, and forced me to heal the broken parts of my soul. You made me stronger and more resilient, and therefore a better person.

Special thanks to my Berlin crew and digital nomad friends who shared so many of my adventures, and taught me the importance of a supportive community of friends.

Last but not least, I want to thank Michelle Pilley and the entire Hay House UK team who believed in this book enough to publish it. It's such an honor and a pleasure to work with you.

I bless you all from the bottom of my heart!

ABOUT THE AUTHOR

Yamile Yemoonyah is an international spirit guide medium and spiritual teacher. She is also the host of The Spirit Guide Show, and founder of the Spirit Guide Society, a community for spiritual seekers, lightworkers, and spiritual activists who want to design a more inclusive, egalitarian, and collaborative world with the help of their spirit guides.

Yamile was in her mid-twenties when a spirit guide physically appeared to her for the first time, and she had no choice but to believe in a reality beyond our 3D world. Since then, she has been on a mission to learn as much as possible about the unseen dimensions of the Universe, especially the myriad forms of conscious beings that inhabit it and how we can communicate with them.

Yamile has helped thousands of people connect with their own spirit guides through private readings, courses, workshops, and her weekly online show.

@yemoonyah

yemoonyah

You Tube Yamile Yemoonyah

TheSpiritGuideMedium.com

Hay House Podcasts
Bring Fresh, Free Inspiration Each Week!

Hay House proudly offers a selection of life-changing audio content via our most popular podcasts!

Hay House Meditations Podcast

Features your favorite Hay House authors guiding you through meditations designed to help you relax and rejuvenate. Take their words into your soul and cruise through the week!

Dr. Wayne W. Dyer Podcast

Discover the timeless wisdom of Dr. Wayne W. Dyer, world-renowned spiritual teacher and affectionately known as "the father of motivation." Each week brings some of the best selections from the 10-year span of Dr. Dyer's talk show on Hay House Radio.

Hay House Podcast

Enjoy a selection of insightful and inspiring lectures from Hay House Live events, listen to some of the best moments from previous Hay House Radio episodes, and tune in for exclusive interviews and behind-the-scenes audio segments featuring leading experts in the fields of alternative health, self-development, intuitive medicine, success, and more! Get motivated to live your best life possible by subscribing to the free Hay House Podcast.

Find Hay House podcasts on iTunes, or visit www.HayHouse.com/podcasts for more info.